The Rose Jar

The Rose Jar

The Autobiography of Edna Meudt

North Country Press
Madison, Wisconsin

North Country Press
3934 Plymouth Circle
Madison, Wisconsin 53705

First Printing
Manufactured in the United States of America

Library of Congress Cataloging-in-Publication Data

Meudt, Edna.
The rose jar.

1. Meudt, Edna—Biography. 2. Poets, American—20th century—Biography. 3. Teachers—Wisconsin—Biography 4. Wisconsin—Biography. I. Title.
PS3525.E84Z476 1990 811′.54 [B] 90-7204
ISBN 0-944133-07-X

Cover photograph by Violet Budoso
Designed by Jane Tenenbaum
Typesetting by Impressions, Inc.
Manufactured by Bookcrafters

CONTENTS

Part IV

FOREWORD

Edna Meudt, who was a dear friend to all who knew her, passed away late in February this year. She was unable to accomplish at least one thing she had wanted in her life. This, she had told me, was to see *The Rose Jar,* her autobiography, published.

On Mother's Day in May, Milwaukee's Woodland Pattern Bookstore held in Edna's memory a reading of her poems. (It is a measure of her vibrancy that this was a day in which Edna herself had been scheduled to read.) During the memorial, listening to others tell their own favorite stories about her, I was struck by the many perspectives that were in the room. It was almost as if we were talking about several different women. Such was her greatness as one of Wisconsin's tribal elders.

Since that day, and perhaps filtered through my own emotions at the memorial, I have come to see that Edna's work deserves to be placed alongside that of Wisconsin writers Zona Gale, August Derleth, Lorine Niedecker and others. It is to say that through a reading of the work of these people, one is able to truly perceive Wisconsin and her folkways.

Eighty-two years before, Edna had been born to immigrant pioneer parents in a blue-frame farmhouse in southwestern Wisconsin's Wyoming Valley. This picturesque township is south of Spring Green, home to *House on the Rock, American Players Theatre* and *Taliesin*, the birthplace of another legendary Wisconsin native, Frank Lloyd Wright. The land here, which millenia ago escaped the last southward incursion of the glacier, is entrancing, with its hills and stone towers suddenly rising from the prairie.

I think that because this land has so much energy residing in it, these two individuals, born forty years apart, were able to translate their first inspiration into a life's work. The powerful land simply had to wait for powerful individuals to celebrate it. Wright began to design a kind of architectural space which was influenced by surrounding natural space. Meudt, whose abilities lived within words, and whose sensibility was tempered by this earth, began during the 1950s to create verse and prose truly reflecting the Wisconsin people and events which had touched her. She wrote of her soulmates, past and present.

Edna was married directly after her graduation from Catholic girl's boarding school in Madison. During the ensuing quarter century, she gave birth to four children, nurtured a farm and family near Dodgeville. She composed her first poem because of the suspected death of a son during World War II. It was published in Chicago's *Poetry Magazine.*

During the next forty years, Edna continued to write of the life around her. Her central works, which she called "The Kristin Poems," are autobiographical, and they portray southwestern Wisconsin in ways no other writer has been able to do. They are intimate and spiritual glimpses into Edna's place on earth, first in the valley, then in the uplands region along Wisconsin's historic Military Ridge. But what makes this poetry unforgettable is that it transcends these particular places. And this was something I think Edna understood clearly —that her most-present life, as Edna Kristin Meudt, was merely one act, one residence through eternity. One can perceive this in poetic accounts such as "Round River Canticle," which are utterly brilliant, incandescent, adventures within the cosmos. They are visions of the center of our being.

I hope you enjoy reading *The Rose Jar* as much as Edna and I enjoyed preparing it.

Jim Stephens
July 10, 1989

Thanks are due the following people who helped put this project together:

Violet Budoso; James Carley; Jean Feraca; Mardi Fries, the literary executor of Edna Meudt's estate; Max Golightly, who graciously read through an early manuscript of *The Rose Jar*; Mark Lefebvre; William Marlin; Jerry Minnich; Betsy Strand; Jane Tenenbaum; and the inestimable George Vukelich of North Country Press. I would like to especially thank Beth and Chris Meudt for their great help in finishing *The Rose Jar* as well as their enormous love and devotion to Edna and her memory.

ACKNOWLEDGMENTS

Some of the stories and poems in this volume have been previously published in the following journals and anthologies: *Heartland Journal, University of Kansas City Review, Wisconsin Academy Review, Wisconsin Trails, A Wisconsin Harvest* (Stanton & Lee, 1966).

A great many of "The Kristin Poems" have been previously published in one or more of Edna Meudt's collections of verse:

Round River Canticle, Wake-Brook House, 1960
In No Strange Land, Wake-Brook House, 1965
No One Sings Face Down, Wisconsin House, Ltd., 1970
The Ineluctable Sea, Wake-Brook House, 1975
Plain Chant For A Tree, Wake-Brook House, 1980

The Rose Jar

Edna in living room, Christmas 1980 (Bruce Fritz photo, Madison Capital Times*)*

Part I

Before Her World

On my front lawn today is a dead cedar covered from base to treetop with bittersweet. From April through summer it is bright green and far more beautiful than when the tree was alive. On into autumn, before the birds have feasted, it wears a grey dress polka-dotted in red. These vines and tendrils are like legends, for they add not only color but dimension, and they take the place of true leaves.

Thus the bittersweet and cedar alike become symbol. It is said that cedar was the wood of the cross. Through legend and by the apprehension of symbols, we learn about those roots of trees hidden away in our sub-conscious. They exist in the nature of our forebears. That is all there is to tell us of faraway homes, the now strange environs, the customs, religion, the lives of the old peoples from whom most of us draw our descent. These trees illumine for us their enculteration.

My grandparents had origin in Europe. From the first their joining was as much a scenario in opposites as cedar and bittersweet. The paternal pair came from the Sumava of Bohemia. Grandfather was a forester who brought his family, including five sons, to Kentucky and then to Wisconsin. He was a pacifist and felt something of the presence of druids in the new country.

No one can now describe Wyoming Valley as it was in 1871, lying between the eastern and western prongs of the trident hills.

The Danish grandfather, Niels Nielson, veteran of the Dano-Prussian and Franco-Prussian wars, plied his trade of roof-thatching. He told his children that heaven is not a place to aspire to, but is the condition of life. The separate beliefs of these men are hearsay. Each of them died before they were fifty years of age. The grandmothers, Mary Marish Kritz and Magdelena Sorenson Nielsen, were widows for thirty years or more.

Now these first bones of my family are calcified, the maps of their days yellowing and in shreds. It is not easy to convince oneself that the reconstruction of skeletons and old maps can be turned into an interesting account. If the reader will but think of this chapter as preparation, as for a meal, or for a new garden, or the fashioning of a garment, then they might acquire faith, as I did, in the outcome. It is as I once wrote in the poem "North Star"—"Oh how well I would listen now" while Mother "told of Danish ways." Kristin's role for her mother, as I wrote then, is "all such midwifery:"

> You would tell of sailing alone for America, this date
> your eighteenth natal day, looking back till Thumbelina-
> sized
> the harbor Mermaid created from Hans Anderson genius
> and Thorvaldsen bronze; of first glimpsing Bartholdi's
> masterwork,
> that Goddess of Liberty born of France's faith in the
> ideal,
> chiseled below with Lazarus' concern for our growing
> pains.

John, my father, one of the five sons of Ignatz Kryz, was brought to America while still an infant. He grew up in sparsely populated and ethnically mixed Wyoming Valley, where it was thought best to Germanize the name to Ignatius Kritz. Had it been anglicized, it would have translated to *Cross*.

When he was seventeen, June 1886, he went to work for

Mother and Father, 1899

the Misses Lloyd-Jones at the Hillside Home School then being built. He was the coachman, not unlike today's limo driver; and the school was three miles from town and the railroad. This was to be a boarding school with an enrollment primarily from Chicago. Summers, the maidens' nephew, came from Madison to help out there or on adjoining uncles's farms. The 1880 census lists under James Lloyd-Jones: "Hired hands: John William Kritz, Frank Lloyd Wright." They shared an upstairs bedroom in the house now known as *Aldebaran*.

During a later period two young men attending Hillside Home School were David and Stanley Gage. Their father was a Chicago lumber magnate. When Stanley was to graduate, he convinced John that he should come to the city and work for his father.

My mother Kristine Nielsen came to America in 1893, the year of Columbian Exposition—that is, Chicago World's Fair. She was expected by the wealthy Shepards of Wilmette, who ran a brokerage. She was a quite beautiful eighteen-year-old, accomplished in homemaking arts. It was worse than demeaning to be assigned as Downstairs Girl.

The Shepards had three daughters who changed attire twice a day, numerous ruffled petticoats, the full regalia. Each Tuesday, Wednesday and Thursday (into the night depending on the number of guests and linens) she sweltered over the pressing board. It was summer and the heavy wrought irons were heated on cast-iron shelves encircling the coal-burning laundry stove. The rest of the weekdays she cleaned.

Good fortune came in the guise of crisis. Important out-of-town company was coming and the cook was very ill. Could anyone fill in? Kristine could and did take over, so well that the cook never got her job back. The pay was nearly double, the work easier and to her liking. Mrs. Shepard was from Paris and had, for that time, exotic recipes which were exciting to one well-versed in Danish cuisine.

Kristine's seven years of service with the Shepards became a happy relationship. While there, she met many prominent people. Years later, introducing a fancy recipe to Valley neighbors, she was not above a little name-dropping. When complimented on a luscious lemon pie taken to the Wyoming Ladies Aid, she was not too modest to say to a newcomer, "I made my first lemon pies for President McKinley's stay at the home where I worked." If urged, she would elaborate: "He was a kind and thoughtful man. His little wife, Ida, was not well. She had lost her only two children while they were young. She carried their photographs in a small velvet bag and would show these, even to us servants. They were darling little girls! She was very dependent and accompanied him wherever he went. It was sad."

With her family and close friends, Kristine shared other details such as: "When the President-elect McKinley (this was 1897) was meeting evenings with prominent Chicagoans, Mrs. McKinley would come out of their room onto the balcony that overlooked the drawing room and call over and over again: 'William! Sweet William! William!' We were told that her children had died at these hours. He would go to her then, speaking most gently, always addressing her as "Mother," not Ida, until she was content to go with Julia, the eldest of the

Shepard daughters, or with one of us. We took turns keeping her entertained or occupied. The help, among ourselves, speculated as to the amount of the bonuses he might give. We were not pleased when he gave us lead pencils with his name stamped in gold." She always beamed when telling that, and she would add: "They'd be worth a pretty penny today! Still, I don't know why we expected anything. Gratuities were not common then, and I enjoyed telling Mrs. McKinley about my life in Denmark. She was so nice! Saying how pretty I was!"

John had been in Wilmette six years, Kristine three, when they met at a baseball game on a spring day in Wilmette Park. They found that they lived only a fair distance apart. They met on the rebound. Each had been engaged to someone else. She, to a Salvation Army Captain named Lawrence, whom she discovered was a womanizer of the first rank.

John's fiancee had simply had second thoughts and changed her mind. Nellie White gave up a very good man. Still, he always held a fondness for a then popular song, "My Darling Nellie Gray." So theirs was not a ready-mix instant romance but a friendship that grew into love that lasted, and she who outlived him maintained—"Beyond the grave!"

Except for John and Kristine's tallness, they were much unalike. He was broody-looking with deepset dark eyes and high cheekbones. His hair was black, as was his groomed moustache. Without any make-up, he could have been the villain in any play.

He loved theatre and opera and the two had their own private small drama. The Gage family, now also in real estate, treated him as one of their own. Certain evenings, he had the use of the carriage and would take Kristine and one of her coworkers to dances. Depending on the season, going to the dance hall or pavilion, the whip would whistle the air as the high-spirited team went snorting up to the entrances.

Kristine loved it and dressed the part—a kind of mystery-lady role. This was the first of their many "arrangements." He never danced or played cards. She had a passion for both. So on those carriage-nights John drove elsewhere to take in a play, an opera or a band concert. When the curtain fell or the concert ended, he came back to where she was, watching and waiting until the orchestra played "Home, Sweet Home."

He was quiet and acquiescent in an often disturbing manner. One knew when he was weighing words and had found them wanting. She was funny and gregarious, but she was also serious and practical with a good business head, of which he was appreciative and from which her family benefited.

After they became engaged, their earnings were pooled and sent to his brother Paul who had himself come to Chicago for several years, but had returned home to purchase, jointly with John, a farm in upper Wyoming. The land was being cleared and a sizeable log building erected. This was to serve first as a home, later as a barn. They were engaged for two years.

It has been wisely said that the anecdote often best illustrates the character. It would be hard to find a better example of the intrinsic differences between John and Kristine than the following: On April 1, 1899, they entrained for Milwaukee to be married. Enroute he told her what the day, April Fools, meant. She refused to go through with the wedding until the next day. No persuasions availed. Later, neither of their children (even when grown) asked about the sleeping arrangements nor how they managed the extra expense.

That April they entered into an agreement (another of Mother's "arrangements") that cast lengthening shadows over their futures and over the lives of their two children-to-be. Their family's background had not originally been homogeneous; Magdalena was Lutheran, Niels Neilsen a non-practicing Calvinist. Kristine was educated in Denmark's parochial schools. John's family was Roman Catholic. Therefore the son born to this union would be raised in his father's faith, the girl, if there was one, in the Lutheran.

After their espousal, for monetary reasons, they stayed on in Wilmette for six months, living mostly apart. Later, of their exodus, Mother would tell this ". . . of their coming to Wyoming Valley:"

His brother Paul was waiting at the depot.
We loaded our belongings in the lumber wagon,

began a trip I'll not forget. At first romantic,
bobbing on the spring seat between such men,
I thought, 'Out here John is all mine.
Nellie will never see him again!'
We came to the Wisconsin River—it looked
like a painting by Constable.
After the river willows and Hillside Colony
we crossed over a ridge of birches and pines,
went into the density of oak-clad bluffs.

So, early in this century there were the parents, John and Kristine, and then their son Leo, at last living in harmony at the upper, southern, end of Wyoming Valley. It would seem to be an idyllic setting, a gentle, believing time, as viewed across eighty-eight years like a riverful of shimmering sunset trails. Slow and quiet and dreamy it was, life there was borderline unbearable for children—ever without perimetry: then as now, neither egg nor chick, neither seed nor plant, but still a growing entity. Consider all those future years of footsteps. What do you see? Childhood is not unlike the nothingness between footfalls. . . .

Leo was almost five when his sister Kristin came to mess up his life. Due to bringing him into being, their mother's heart was damaged. She could not forget, that he was overdue, oversize—all boney angles and jaundiced, a colicky baby who cried every night. Kristin, on the other hand, came as one to whom atonement was due. (The attending physician had foiled their fear-filled attempts to abort her.) She came in an easy birth, looking like a real live Rose O'Neill Kewpie. Who can imagine how often Leo must have looked on that sister, in her cradle a living doll, and thought: "I won't have that creature around!"

Soon after her first birthday, Kristin contracted polio. So now, in that home haunted by dogmas of a vengeful god, there were fresh fears of a retribution, that she might be taken from them, for, added to her cherubic presence, she became doubly precious and humored. Unable to walk until the age of three, she had poor Leo ever at her beck and call. All this before her discovery of flowers and kittens, of birds seen in flight and animals heard at dawn . . . before longing began, and while she was still called "Little Kristin."

Told of Indian Summer

From Sumava where the Moldau begins, to Kentucky The Dark and Bloody Land, my father's people in the early 1800s brought their legends. Hidden behind the wilderness of the Alleghenies before the vedettes of civilization looked from the Cumberland Mountains westward over her silent forests, it was a region much like the Home of the Boli from which they came. Here also was a country where ages had passed since the Mound Builders vanished, leaving along the rivers and plateaus great fortresses to haunt the newcomers with their mysteries.

A kinship was established with the sturdy mountaineers, who like themselves were mostly tall and angular of frame, with strong features, and intelligence marked with an innate sadness. Even so, their gypsy blood stirred and within three decades they moved on to the newly designated Wisconsin Territory.

My father said that footsteps of humans were not common when he was a boy. But everywhere in the uppermost ravines of their valley were animals and fowl that multiplied freely. The deep clear streams teemed with fish and muskrat. In the sky, above the comb of the forest upland to the south, sailed some of the smaller eagles and all the families of hawks. "But," he said, "there were fewer songbirds in those days though many more than now." He was then in his seventies.

Near a place where the wagon trail came from the woods and crossed the creek, my father and two of his brothers were fishing one day when a man came along in such a rig as they had never seen before. Father, lying on his belly with his shirt off, was trying to catch with his bare hands the trout that hide under ledges. He was so startled that, wearing only the homespun pants Baba had made, he jumped into the water to hide. He was about ten, Lew and Frank just a few years older.

The man whoaed his team to a halt and got down from the seat and loosened reins so the horses could drink. He stood very erect like a soldier. As far as the boys knew there was no war going on. All the same they were uneasy, having heard tales of boys taken against their will. Grandfather, who had been brought to America to escape Prussian militarism, always impressed on his sons the horrible aspects of war and slavery:

"When you were a baby, John, the most frightful human we ever saw came to us. He was a black man who had not been outside the saltpetre cavern in how many years he did not know. Our Baba used poultices of yellow dock and jimson seed on his sores and in less than a week he went on his way." There were many such stories of sick and maimed soldiers during and after the war. It was soon after that father moved the family to this hidden valley. "We can follow the ways of peace here," he said.

Now the stranger stood staring down at Father, who came up shivering out of the water. When the man spoke it was sharply:

"How'd you big lazy fellows like to earn some money? Huh?"

Uncle Lew, being the eldest of the trio, dared to explain that they were getting fish while the water was still cold, to salt and dry for the next winter. He told the brothers afterward how he hoped the man would want to buy some. But all the man did was to snatch up their prize catch, a rainbow trout, and throw them a penny each. And they did not dare to protest that the trout was best for winter storing and was not for sale.

"You backwoods fellows ever hear of fish without any eyes? Huh? Well there are! In a grotto near Litchton, Kentucky." The man held their eighteen inch trout with both hands and squeezed it behind the gills. "Well this one sure got eyes."

Father said he wished that beautiful fish alive again and hiding along the creek bank. And that it took him several years to forget the experience when he caught a trout.

The stranger put the fish in the rear of his high, closed wagon and pulled out a large, woven bag. He then strode up front and jerked the horses' heads from the grass they were nibbling and snapped the checkreins to the girthband. He went back and got the bag he had set on the ground. "Peanuts," he said, "Enough to plant an acre or more." Seeing their interest he told them how to spade the new sod and plant the peas. "You'll see how the blossoms lean into the ground. Let them alone. That's how you get the peanuts," he said.

The boys were hard workers for their years. Even in the woods they often took the heavy load, for something was not right with their father's lungs. However, Grandfather was the expert at peeling and hewing the timbers for railroad ties which he took to town in winter—15 miles on a sled. They had other wearisome chores but they knew about peanuts: their only near neighbor, Sam Bradley, the autumn he was moving Out West, brought them a bag of this product, new to their country store. So, added to the lure of earned-money was the thought of such a treat to brighten their winter fare. They worked the peanut patch with diligence and it thrived.

Grandfather, coming from a line of millers and foresters knew about many crops, and of the harvesting of these. But before this one was ready he fell fatally ill. He was the first to lie in the pretty place where the red oaks gleamed like green temples, and where he and Baba, looking to the future, had envisioned a new house. There was no one to read from the Bible over him, nor from the Prophecies of Libuse' that he like so much. He had spoken English well, Baba only the few basic words. Lew stood with his mother, the other sons led the prayers in Bohemian. Mary, Annie and Emma sang a Stephen Foster hymn. And when their mother asked them all to sing "Going Home," his favorite, it was the boys who could not finish for weeping.

Already the shadows were lying long across the meadow. The woods were flooding in yellow and maroon when the spring stranger returned. Soon he was shouting that they were all "Lazy lummoxes too stupid to know enought to dig a crop when it was ready." This was in the morning and he stayed the whole day ordering them: "Get on with it. Hurry! Hurry!"

The entire family worked, even Baba who was carrying her tenth child that was soon to be buried beside her husband. My father who lived by a rule that "Our kindlier judgements are our better judgements" was acid-tested when he spoke to us of what went on that day.

Peanuts dug and the loading done, the man jumped onto the seat of that rig and was off. He left them several bushels as well as the stragglers around the edges of the patch that were still to be gotten out of the ground. And he gave each boy only one silver dollar.

They knew the trader had wronged them, but not how meanly until they tried to eat the nuts. Not only was there no one to tell them about storage, they did not know that unroasted peanuts are inedible. Many had spoiled before a young man, engaged in taking the census, arrived at their farm in time for supper. Seeing their predicament, and being weary, he stayed the night. Together, the next morning, they salvaged those that were still good, some to save for seed, the others for roasting. It was their first contact with the world outside their valley in nearly three months. He brought them news of the presidential election controversy between Tilden and Hayes, disquieting words about the trouble in Louisiana and the military occupation there. But the memorable story he brought (and the point of mine) was about a trader. They all agreed it must have been the same one with whom they had dealt:

A man driving a team hitched to a high rig stopped one evening at the smelting furnace on the Old Lead Road that led from Galena to the Shot Tower on the Wisconsin River. He had passed that way months before, it was said, going the opposite direction. There were suspicions about the cargo then, as well as his business with the Sioux. So on the return he made camp at the furnace and started the slow-roasting of a load of peanuts he must have been planning to sell along the way to wherever it was he belonged. After sun-up and while he still slept some young Indians came by. It was thought they had been drinking and must have recognized him as one who had cheated, and cursed at their people. They left him for dead but he was still alive when another wayfarer came past. The trader was able to gasp out what had happened to him there.

Father would always ask us then: "And do you suppose we were glad when we heard about that man?" He was disappointed if any child, or grandchild, could think that those time-distant children were happy for such an ending. Then he would continue: "Our Baba never did learn the words, Indian Summer. For that season of the year she used Bohemian words that translated meant, 'Strange man roasting peanuts.' "

We used to never tire of hearing him say those funny-sounding words which I can repeat though I cannot spell them. While we were young, when he spoke that phrase, he sniffed the air and asked: "Don't you like the Indian Summer name better? You should because we are Americans."

All the same, when I was a child, and the Uplands were a smoky blue, maples and larches turning gold as fire, I could distinctly smell the freshly roasted peanuts. Sometimes.

Tornado and Flood

Memory is a concave crystal through which the past may sometimes be viewed; it is inward-curved, hollow, at first, an empty nest. Forgotten episodes emerge, as long as our bodies have not tired of us nor our wits forsaken us. Such remembrances add dimension to our reveries; they are so integral to the psyche as should have been unforgettable. The remembrances which may have been beyond recall now come back in snatches and snippets, evanescent, often as not, triggered by irrelevancies.

Are not such glimpses as through a concave lens? (The opposite being convex, curving outward. That mode, on the other hand, is of expectations, the future.) Since we cannot run at childhood's pace, nor function in the worlds of our maturity forever, much more of the energy of memory leaks out than will return to our present. And the clutter is there, as we look into haunted and shadowed caverns.

But how much do we remember as having experienced — or as having been told to us? It may be both, a combo playing its inside music—the actual event slurred and muted; or a surrealist pattern, as when Kristin fancies herself recall a dreamlike day during her second spring, in June of 1908.

Thursday afternoons in Wyoming Valley were for visiting

Kritz Family, Wyoming Valley, May 1910

in the homes of neighbors. Sundays, after church services, they talked in little groups, and in pleasant weather there were impromptu potluck picnics. These were times when communication was in somewise important as nourishment.

On such a Thursday, Mother and Leo were going to call on Ole and Jane Ann Paul, whose young sons were Ernest, Earl and Laurence. The afternoon was unseasonably warm so Mother took her silk parasol. They would go through a small piece of woods and a clean pasture, a bit more than a half-mile walk.

Father was fencing the garden with high woven wire that would keep the poultry out, the strawberries were ready, the currants reddening. Kristin would take her nap on a folded comforter under the square oak table used for trimming rhubarb and vegetables for the compost pile.

"No sense carrying all that foliage to the house and then back again," Mother said that morning. She draped mosquito netting over the table, kissed Father and went off with Leo.

Kristin, who had fallen asleep to lullabies of orioles and bluebirds and to sounds made by post-maul and hammer, wakened to a strange silence and gloom. This was not mere darkness. Far, far away there were rumblings of the sort Shep made deep in his throat, when daring the cats to come near his food. Kristin lay very still, listening. Even though Father was nowhere to be seen, she did not cry. It was as though she had been born knowing such hullabaloo was unseemly—as Father sometimes said.

She sat up. Where were the birds? And the pretty roosters with their talkative ladies? Father came out of the toolshed, sat on the grindstone frame and looked up at the sky. Comforted, Kristin heard the rumbling grow louder, then a wind lifted the netting and carried it off.

After that the onslaught! She would recall that frightful noise afterward when Father was sick and they took him on a train with an engine that made such sounds. She found herself being pulled roughly from under the table. Father was running with her away from the trees, toward the barn, into which he threw them both.

The film of this remembrance snaps there but she remembers vividly a whirring as from dragonflies.

Sixty years later she wrote of this in a poem. Her friend, August Derleth, said: "Before I can publish this we have to change: *I lay under my father while tornado and flood / robbed us of all but life*. In this gravelly age," he said, "we have to say: *I lay half underneath my father*."

He was right. That was in the sixties, the first probings into drainage channels, treacherous with its gasefied pockets of child abuse and incest. Headline stuff better suited to the bottoms of compost heaps! It has brought us, sadly, to a public condition when conscientious, loving parents hesitate to show affection, or to discipline their young. While concern over air and water is indeed importunate, little attention is paid to the fouling of the emotional climate in our lives.

The climate of Wyoming Valley was erratic that summer, for after the coming of the tornado, there were weeks of drought. After the dry-spell, which lasted through the growing season, came the deluge; the large valley creek overflowed its banks, and still it rained. In newly-formed ditches and gullies, debris from woods and pastures washed down to the main stream. Under the big wooden bridge, on the town road below the barn, floods had dammed the water to the west.

It was as watertight, Father said, as if a colony of beavers had been at work. He knew, given time, the town board would see to opening the waterway under the bridge. He also saw that the water was washing deep ruts in the road and backing up into the cow-yard. All the neighbors had this problem in some degree. "The Lord helps those who help themselves," he had quoted that morning at breakfast. "If more rain comes, we're in real trouble. I'll see what I can do."

Leo asked, "Can I stay home and work with you?"

"You may not," Mother said. "There'll be enough days in winter when you have to miss school. I'll help."

And Kristin said, "I'll help." Everyone laughed except Kristin.

Leo took his dinner pail and left for school. Mother cleared the breakfast table, carried Kristin to the summer cabin, put her into the high wicker buggy. The morning was bright with sun but there was a fast breeze from the east. The lawn and grassy roadside were spongy and they went slowly. "You are getting too big for this buggy," Mother said, wheeling Kristin onto the bridge. "Mind you, sit quietly and look at your picture books."

Kristin promised. There was shade from the willows and a few birds were about but mainly the strange, insistent calls of the jays held her attention. She decided to not look at the black, bad-smelling water.

Father came leading the mare with the whiffletree and rope used for pulling the laden hayfork up to the track and on into the barn. On one arm he carried a heavy chain. Soon he was into the water up to his armpits, looping the chain around some branches farthest away from the bridge.

Mother, on the bank, led the mare; Father pulled at and loosened others. They worked steadily for a couple of hours, but still had not made a breakthrough.

"We're getting there!" Kristin heard Father say. "The water is quite deep here." He was closer to the bridge now, out of her view.

Then Mother said, "All this water and not a drop to drink. Let's rest a bit."

"See to Kristin," said Father, "and I'll get us some water from the spring."

The sun was high above the trees, the shade gone. Mother turned the carriage, took the ruffled parasol from its compartment above the axletrees and fastened it firmly into its socket. She opened it, facing about to meet Father, who was coming with the jug of water. A gust of wind caught in the muslin parasol and rolled the buggy over the edge and into the water. Mother screamed and fainted.

Father always said: "There was but one decision. Your mother was given to fainting spells. A drowned child cannot be brought back."

Judging from the way he darkened when speaking, it was a very bad matter: "You were trapped under the carriage and it was caught among the rubbish. I called on God with a loud voice, I promised Him everything I could think of. And then I found your foot in that black depth and God gave me strength to move what I could not have budged under ordinary circumstance."

At first thought, Kristin was dead . . . "And then you coughed a little of that filthy water up and I held you over my arm with your head down and patted your back. More water came up and you began to whimper."

There was also more to the account: "Oh I was glad for having worked at Hillside Home School, for what I'd learned being at the Wisconsin River with the students. Otherwise I might have despaired—given you up."

Mother revived on her own and took charge: "He had forgotten me!"

"And I," Father said, "stood there sobbing so loudly the neighbors could have heard. I could not quit shaking, even in the house, while your mother bathed you."

"Talking to himself like his mind was gone!"

"No," Father said, "I was praying my thanks to almighty God."

"It was I who had to be practical and send him to get the mare loose and ready the driving horses for the trip to the doctor," she said. "You were scraped and bruised. I was worried about bones having been broken and a lump on your forehead."

This was Kristin's third brush with death, her last exposure to the elemental cruelty of the world. There would be three more close calls before she was nine, which would mark her for life.

This was no handed-down memory. It was there every time she looked into deep water, a queasiness, a cold sweat and usually a spell of graphic dreams in which she was immersed all night, not just a few minutes.

Kristin would write of this in a number of poems, but not until putting down these words did she realize that water had been the bond with her father—perhaps an even stronger one than the amniotic one with Mother. Strange!

Sacraments

Mother was practical and pragmatic. The closest town was Spring Green, ten miles away, so it was understood that they could not participate in religious services every Sunday, especially in winter. That spring and summer when Kristin was to be four in September, more and more they were going to Mother's church. Almost never were they attending Sunday Mass. Occasionally Father mentioned this to Mother, but nothing changed. That is, not until September, in 1910.

Clearly this is an inconstant memory of a time beyond Kristin's emotional grasp, until years later. Its harvest was insight: love and power, and the larger collection of truths: TRUTH!

Father was ailing that summer. He did not eat well. Even Mother's stewed hen with Danish dumplings, for which she was lauded beyond the Valley, no longer appealed to him. Soon the stomach sickness worsened; he coughed and retched far into the nights. Then he wanted no food, only fresh water from the spring. The well water tasted like quinine, he said, as he took a little honey on his tongue.

Worst of all for Kristin was that he did not look like Father anymore, so thin, and hollow around the eyes. When he smiled, which was seldom, there was no light in their brown depths.

Two doctors were involved in Father's situation; neither

could be sure, but they thought, they said, that this was the result of an undetected injury at the time of the tornado. During the incident, logs rolling over him as he protected Kristin beneath him, had broken his shoulder and maybe some ribs. Or that following winter when he misjudged its span, the branch of a falling tree had struck his chest?

Once, on the way home, Kristin heard him say to Mother: "What difference does the cause make? I'm in my forties, nearing the same age as my father was when he died of stomach cancer."

Kristin, listening from her bed that night, heard the rest: "I can take the pain. It's leaving you and the children I can't bear." Through an open register near where Kristin lay, the clock downstairs struck a high number and set her to trembling. Their voices were muffled and she thought they might be crying. She also wept.

Later, having witnessed many deaths from varieties of cancers, she understood better what he was saying. In his father's terrible torture, few of the pain-alleviating drugs were known. In her father's time of trial this had changed very little. It was a brave statement on his part, and true. For him, the only pain he found hard to bear was that inflicted on others.

Grave and far-reaching decisions were to be made. Father would go to Madison General Hospital where Dr. Keenan, a specialist, was to perform the surgery. The prognosis was gloomy.

Because Mother loved him, she had to set their house in order. First, the "arrangement" which for ten years had seemed to proceed in so reasonable a course, had to be looked at for what it was: sinful and heretical. In 1910, according to Catholic Doctrine, having been married by a justice of the peace, they were *not* married. They were "living in sin." Almost as bad: they had an unbaptized child who, had she died, could "never enter Heaven and would languish through all eternity in a state known as Limbo."

The situation called for scrutiny: Mother, going along with the agreement that Leo should be Catholic, had chosen for him the name "Fremont" after an American General and explorer.

This man was a hero in the Shepard home, where Mother had gone to work on coming to America.

The name "Fremont" and Leo's birthdate she recorded in the Bible brought from Denmark. However, the pastor in Spring Green would have no part in such "heathenism." Catholic babies were named for saints! He suggested "Leo" and "Benedict," who were two papal saints. (It is very easy to conjure up the outrage within this Lutheran-Calvinist mother.) She refused to participate in that caricature of a christening.

Soured though she was, she had discussed the baptism of Kristin with Rev. Nestande, her minister, and with another Protestant clergyman, Rev. Shoenfeldt. Neither of these men would reinforce her conviction that "baptism is necessary for salvation."

So Mother went to Dodgeville, where Father's mother, sister Annie and brother Paul lived, all members in good standing at St. Joseph's Parish: Father Andrew Ambauen was from Switzerland, a scholar and a poet. "Yes!" he agreed with Mother, "Baptism is a must!" He must have been far ahead of his time to have sized up the condition so compassionately: the beautiful, troubled wife of a man mortally ill.

He waived all requirements for pre-nuptial instructions and said he would rectify their marriage and baptize their child the next Sunday, after Mass. The bridesmaid and best man served as Kristin's godparents. Almost fearfully, Mother enquired if "Edna," the new name they wanted for Kristin, was a saint's name? "If it isn't," Father Ambauen answered, "we'll make it one!"

And he poured the waters and called her "Edna Kristin" and he gave her a new silver dollar. To Mother, he gave a solid walnut carving of *The Lion of the Helvetians*, a copy, done in Switzerland, of Thorvaldsen's masterpiece. Mother prized it all her life. Each year Kristin rejoices in it more and more.

Growing up and grown, the child and woman who was Kristin always liked the first given name better. When she began to express her life in writing, it surfaced again—gradually it did so. In her mind and in her poems and stories will she always remain—Kristin.

First Journeys

Circumstances made getting used to a new name quite simple. That and the reasons for the change which have been explained earlier: Father said, "Your mother is Kristine. Soon you won't be Little Kristin anymore. You will grow up to be a woman and you must not be a shadow of someone else." He had held her close and his breath was such she was glad to get down and go her lonely way.

Mother said, "With a name like mine, sometimes they shorten it to 'Tina.' We are very tall people. Wouldn't you hate that? And folks laughing?"

Likely the excitement, the emotional stress coupled with physical exertions, brought matters to crisis. The morning after the incidents in Dodgeville, Father got up as usual. All he took for breakfast was a cup of hot water. Mother coaxed until he said, yes, he would like some lemon pie, especially with a high meringue, but he couldn't promise he would eat the crust.

Humming to herself, Mother got out all the makings, saying to her newly-named little girl, "So it will be cool and firm for an early lunch." Father had gone outside to tend the chickens and to do a few other light chores.

Two pies, one lemon and one apple, were cooling in the pantry. Kristin had gotten to "lick" the filling and meringue pans and all was right in her world. Father had not come in, so Mother went to the door and called. Kristin went out with her to look when he did not answer. They found him lying on his side, barely able to speak. A trickle of blood came out the side of his mouth, and on the ground it looked to Kristin like a slice of beet pickle.

Here is remembered only Mother's telling. "Providentially, within a few minutes Ernie Paul came by, going for the mail." Ernie was a neighbor boy of about fifteen. "He was horseback and he rode as Sigurd must have ridden, through fire, so quickly he brought help." Later, Kristin remembered that Mother always had a culinary treat for Ernie.

Uncounted are all the leaf-filled autumns, uncharted the rutted roads since that day. The early fears and anxieties have consumed themselves. There are no traces of the blood and the anguish except in memory. Across half a century, thousands of pies later, Kristin, renamed Edna, grates the lemons lightly, as her mother did, lest the filling be bitter.

And on any Fall day when light glances on dying leaves as over water, that trip to town comes clearly in retrospect. As with the poems she wrote years later, the one called "First Journey," became that journey, indelibly. Along with the tragic fire at Taliesen five years later, this experience was far-reaching and left deep scars.

She had known life-threatening illness firsthand, and had been the center of concern. While Father was ailing, she was aware but not alarmed. Then came the excitement of that christening, and Mother and Father getting married . . . again. Sunday, and on its heels, Father lying beside the grindstone, looking *dead.* The farm child comes to grips with death, livestock and pets, even before propagation is witnessed. No "baby sitters" or squeamishly sparing children the trauma, in those days, in that place.

The situation was handled promptly and well, as was to be expected of self-reliant good neighbors. Ernie brought back Ole and Jane Ann, his parents, and Bertha, an eighteen-year-old sister. All but Ernie helped to make the light wagon as comfortable as possible, then they loaded Father into it as if he were

Leo, Mother and Grandmother Kritz

going to market. Ernie had gone on ahead immediately to have Doc Watson hold the train if need be, and afterward, to drive the team back to the farm. Bertha would stay with Leo to run the place. Father was conscious and calm. He wanted only Mother and Kristin to accompany him.

The drive to Spring Green was scary enough! Then the monstrous train (the Chicago, Milwaukee and St. Paul's finest) stood huffing and puffing, and people had gathered about. When they carried Father into it, Kristin was sure that this time the end, for her, was at hand. But it was beautiful inside, red velvet like the cape sent by Cousin Marie and lamps the color of stars.

Then there was the noisy car-vehicle that waited their arrival to take them to Madison City Hospital. The conductor had telegraphed ahead. Many were the occasions later when men were helpful and caring. Kristin would remember that fine-looking man with gold braid and shiny buttons, and sensed it was no handicap being a lovely woman, when in distress.

At the hospital, Kristin sat alone for a long time, frightened and hungry. Forgotten. Then a man came into the front room and saw her sitting there solemn as a barred owl. He was dressed all in black and his white collar had no necktie. She guessed he was a priest like Father Ambauen who had baptized her. When he came and sat on the chair next to her and spoke gently and smiled, she began to cry. He pretended not to notice and to be admiring her picture Bible. It felt so good to have met a friend! Soon he moved away from her and talked with a lady dressed in stripes with a snowy white apron and bonnet. The lady looked toward Kristin and smiled and hurried away. When she came back she carried a glass of milk and a plate with three raisin cookies. The handsome young man, whose name was Father Doyle, said that he must go and see the sick people, and that he would see her again.

Mother and Kristin settled in at the house where they would stay while Father was in the hospital. Kristin supposed it would be overnight, such as when they went to Dodgeville to see Baba and slept at Aunt Annie's, but it was not to be so.

The house was Mrs. O'Connell's. She was a widow who had raised her family almost alone by taking in roomers. Her youngest, a son named Jack, was still at home to help. He was Irish and to Kristin he looked very good. That first night he brought a bowl of apples, plums and grapes to their small room. When Kristin knew him better, she told him that she had not expected to find fruit trees and big gardens. Jack said that once all of Milton Street had been fruit farms and truck gardens: "All the way over to the lake and where those big University buildings now stand."

"What did you do with all that food?" Kristin asked, and Jack laughed and said, "Well, that was before my time. There were soldiers camped over there (he pointed toward Camp Randall) and they had to be fed. There was a war going on, but you wouldn't know about that."

"The Civil War?" she asked, surprising him. And then she told him about their sometimes neighbor, old Uncle Eric, who was in that war. From then on they were friends.

Jack took her to her first movie. The building was almost finer than the train, especially on the inside, all trimmed in gold, and seats with soft arms.

Then the movie began, showing first a big snake in trees, where it went from one to another tree; she did not like it, but it was interesting. In Wyoming Valley, the snakes were smaller and stayed on the ground. Soon bears and lions appeared to be coming right out of the picture and toward them. She ran screaming from the theatre. Jack retrieved her, reassuring her, and with some coaxing she went back in, feeling safe with her hand in his.

As truly as O. E. Rolvaag represented in his classic, there were *giants in the earth* living there on the edge of the "Greenbush" section of Madison. Jack O'Connell later got in on the ground floor of utilities and became so successful that the mansion he built in Maple Bluff is now historically significant. Another was Leo Crowley, who was to help President Franklin Roosevelt rebuild America's ruined finances.

And there was a ten-year-old boy living at 1013 Milton Street, who was to become not only a well-known athlete but a Latin and Greek scholar as well. He was handsome and charismatic. He became a priest, slated for position in the Catholic hierarchy, had he not met Kristin nineteen years later.

Father was very ill. At first Dr. Kennan did not hold out much hope that he would recover and Mother stayed with him as long as was permitted by the hospital. When he was improving, and Mrs. O'Connell was busy with other roomers and Jack was working, Kristin went to the hospital also.

There was Father Doyle, in a sense a prevision of the love of Kristin's maturity. She had not met the new pastor in Spring Green, where her family would go to church: Father John Brudermanns, as much as any other (perhaps *more* than any other since he was the *first*) who would shape her literary life. And the boy then living on Milton Street would change her entire life.

It was the time of one scarring experience of which she was never to be rid, one never to be put out of her young mind, it was that painful. Conversely, in youth and maturity, its value was beyond estimation. Kristin, not born with a contemplative nature, but sentenced by polio to early practice of inner living (and because of geography oriented to loneliness), profited much sooner than most children from the home environment of a biased mother and a non-judgmental father.

During one of the meetings with Father Doyle, he took her to the garden in back of the hospital. There were fruit trees and lovely flowers and a few benches with tables, a place where relatives could come for relief from whatever worries they had. Kristin was a well-mannered girl, though much experience with sickness had made her old for her years. Father Doyle liked her company and they spent hours together.

As later, when she was allowed to roam the woods as she pleased, Mother paid little attention to where she was. One day, straining too hard to pick a branch of bright-red crabapples to bring her father, her garter-pin broke open and tore a long gash to her knee. It bloodied her white stocking and Father Doyle unfastened the garter tabs and rolled the stocking down. When they went in search of a nurse, they met Mother on the stairs. Her reaction was ferocious. The horror tales of her upbringing surfaced, of priests being emissaries of the devil. During her Chicago years, she had read a yellow newspaper called *The Menace*. The "Menace" was the Pope and the paper was full of gory tales of orphanages full of the offspring of priests and nuns. Kristin did not know this Mother. She looked up into the face of the dear man who had been so kind to her and she could not say a word. Neither did he speak a word in defense. Details of the episode are in the poem "First Journey." It took many years, filled with pain and joy, before she could write the ending to this situation:

Grow child! Accept loss;
come to terms with shamed innocence and injustice;

take up position in council and battlement;
become sum total of all that was,
with mind a potter's field over which memory glides
like night birds, searching the infinitesimal.

Forget where you came at sun
and savored the tears of loves begun,
but linger where the faraway rhythm
of hooves and riverwash and early owl
counterpoints a luminous spiritual
in mountain ash and appled hawthorn.
Treasure all that ramparts the knowing heart
and gives eyes for back of mirrors,
ears deaf to defilement;
a tongue with delicacy for truth.

There may be some who protest: "Oh, but she turned Catholic, she embraced his faith." Yes, she was a "rice convert;" her bowl of rice was the assurance that her husband's spiritual life was in order so that, had he died, they could be reunited in the afterlife. Did she outgrow these prejudices? Not so. During the Edgewood period, when she dared, Kristin sometimes expressed her attraction to the religious life of the Dominicans. "I would rather see you dead!" was Mother's stock reply, and Leo and Kristin had reason to believe she meant what she said. How often they had nudged each other knowingly when the pastor made disparaging remarks about those red herrings of Catholicity, Martin Luther and John Calvin! Brother and sister knew there would be mild fireworks on the way back to Wyoming Valley in the afternoon.

It was Leo who perceived that such deeply-rooted aversions had more than a little to do with Mother's urgency to "marry her off" only four months after Edgewood. (Engaged since she was fifteen, she had been promised a year's time before marriage.) "She's afraid you'll run away to the convent and become a nun," Leo said. "You better believe I've heard the talk. And don't expect Dad to stand up to her. He can't anymore."

During long nights when sleep still did not come easily, she pondered the matter and was dutiful and acquiescent; neither fish nor fowl, as the saying goes. What she didn't know was that she was nurturing strengths and insights; those religious arguments taught her there had to be rights and wrongs on both sides. Somewhere in the middle, in between, there would be compromise, a sound solution?

In the mornings, those last summers of her girlhood, she could see the lily bed outside her room, which, in a poem, she called "a riddle in the round." Mother had planted the bulbs and tubers in circles and the bed bloomed continuously from spring into September, with pasque flowers, through amaryllis, through turk's-cap.

Then, in autumn, they all slept together, growing their strengths for the future, for another spring. It was an immature concept, "sufficient for the evil thereof." That did not resolve her inner conflict about imminent marriage, but it imparted a semblance of peace and acceptance.

Without such experience she could not have written in full maturity, meaning every line:

There emerged from the anonymous past
an awareness that I was, like Uriah Heep,
proud of humility, and in charity wanting
for failure to cherish the ways of her who bore me.

A dreamer, beguiled with idealism,
I questioned her austerity, excused and tolerated
in others the characteristics she could not change:
the Reformation fused in her an essence
that marked her children for insight
as simply as joy is born of sorrow.

My Mother, loosed now of creeds
and from Self released to inviolable peace—
thinking on you,
wind's sign away but separate, as shadow,
I see you paused in the dooryard,
praying for kinfolk oceans afar.

Your voice and hardened hands are gentled
by loneliness few could comprehend.
Across the island universe, across the years,
Mother,
your child's appreciation of paradox.

Sooner than she might have thought, the September day came when she was five. She started off to school—a princess going to her palace, where there is only peace and pretty rooms and no goblins from that "other world." Leo was tall and lean and swift-moving, as were the neighbor brothers, ten and eleven. There was no malice in their neglect, merely indifference. The distance was two miles over a steep hill. She did not know that they were walking the legs out from under her, or she would have tattled on them.

At the top of the hill one day, there was the taste of blood in her mouth and throat, as when she put a cut finger to her lips. She thought to mention this, but there was her "piece to speak" for the pre-Thanksgiving program. Her mind was mostly on this important event! The piece was "Twinkle, Twinkle, Little Star" and she practiced in bed each night when stars were to be seen. Nothing must interfere, she knew, with that performance—though later, short of breath and falling down the steps from the stage in disgrace, she wished something had!

Light no longer played on the ripples, the creek was frozen over. It was December. Stoically, in heavy woolens and astrakhan collarette, she trudged along after the boys, till one day she stopped, stood still and announced that she was going to sleep on that frozen hill. Her breath came as through a slippery-elm whistle, heaving and whittling her insides.

Half carrying her, taking turns, the three boys got her home, where they were scolded for their neglect. For that, Kristin was sorry. It wasn't anybody's fault, it was everybody's fault. It had not come on all at once, the doctor said.

The fainting couch was moved from the parlor into the dining room where a kettle was kept steaming on the Round Oak stove. Father was near frantic. For a week he slept on fur robes beside the couch. The doctor called her sickness "lung fever."

The eye of that "tornado" passed but the storm was still lowering. Unknown to Kristin, a ghost had come into their home. Frances, Father's young sister, who had gifts of clairvoyance, had truly died of lung fever. She had foreseen her funeral cortege less than a week before she died. In that somber household, Leo walked the straight and narrow, seldom speaking unless spoken to. By Christmas, the clouds were lifted.

The plus of the minus winter was that Father took them to school with team and sleigh. When Kristin was permitted to go, and only on cold days, he or Ernie Paul came for them after school.

Seventh Summer

Kristin studied the clock in the kitchen as if it were in Mr. Hathaway's Shop window where coveted things were displayed. It would be several hours before Mother, Father and Leo would come down from the hill fields with a hayrack towering with fragrant clover. Mother was up there raking the overripe timothy which would be stacked for steers and horses that wintered out.

Kristin's chores were almost finished: the dinner dishes were washed and dried, ten quarts of canned strawberries had been carried to the root cellar, the peas were picked for supper. She could have puttered the whole afternoon away at these, had Mother been home to find extra jobs, but alone in the house, she worked with purpose.

Outside again, she squinted to see where the sun was in relation to the big hill where, in afternoons, the sun sank down. Teacher said this was not so, that the sun stayed put and the world was turning. She had rather not bother herself about that. The always present awareness was to know when to come home from the woods. She called Shep. When he did not come, she realized he must be on the ridge with Leo.

"A summer day for hummers" she sang, passing the honeysuckle vine where a hummingbird hovered. Bees and insects

Edna, Father and Mother

were in the air and around the trumpet vine were two larger hummers. Portly roosters were out walking their harems. She missed their spring races and mountings, none of which meant more to her than the calves racing around the orchard. "I mustn't forget to gather the eggs. And get back in time to shell the peas for supper," she said, making other observations aloud to herself.

Crossing the creek at the shallows, she stood awhile, shoes in hand, letting the mellow water soothe some nettle welts on her ankles. She wished Shep were along so they could splash each other. It was a game of which they were both fond. She stood alone listening to riffles, no "lop lop lop lops" from Shep drinking, no scolding squirrels in the oaks. Alone.

She stopped to rest at the mulberry tree growing at the edge of the woods, tasted some of the fallen fruit, bland after having all the strawberries one could eat. It was a kind of sharing, a partaking with the dear birds.

Twice, near sundown, Leo had brought her here and they could not count the numbers and kinds of birds that came to feed. Years after, when waiting in travel terminals, seeing the men in drab garb, the women and children in brighter attire, she could almost recapture the sweetness of those sundowns under the mulberry, for one had to lie perfectly still on the shady side where no fruit had fallen. Today not more than a dozen came and went, and because of bothersome insects it was hard not to brush them away.

On the path into the deep woods she picked gerardia, rose-pinks and sweet william, put these in two bouquets under the tallest pine. Her quest this day was for the late white lady's slippers in their swampy hideaway, their fragrance permeating the air before they could be seen. The excitement of this moment was the same as last year when Mother had found them.

Thinking how surprised and pleased Mother would be, she ran and knelt at the edge of the patch and kissed as many as could be reached. Mother had picked only a dozen because, she had exclaimed, "These are very rare!" Kristin took fifteen, planning to stuff three with cotton wool to be dried in the attic for her room. More were left than she had taken.

Sitting on a fallen branch under a honey locust, she was

arranging them so no bloom came too close together, when she heard what she thought was Martin Johnson's old, worn-out team of sorrels. Dry brush was breaking as they came closer. She turned to look, and saw that the presence was taller than Father and as black as his Sunday suit, only this apparition was shiny, glistening black like the fishing holes in the creek, wore no shirt and its hair was crinkly like the ram that had to be sold because no fence could hold him.

The mouth and eyes of whatever this presence was rooted her in terror. The teeth were like those of the stallion which was brought to their place in late spring, and about which the grown-ups were secretive. The horse's eyes seemed partly white like this black creature's, who was now quite close. She was unable to move or make a sound. Then she knew that this was a man. The man was black, the first she had ever seen.

Her first lesson that Black is beautiful! For now the man saw her. He stopped in his tracks and his big eyes got even bigger. "Lord Jesus!" he said, and he turned and moved slowly away from her and never looked back.

While he walked away, her frozen insides thawed, breath returned and she got to her feet. Abandoned were the showy lady's-slippers and wildflower bouquets as she ran, faster than Shep would have over rocks and fallen branches, through brambles and thorny bushes, past the mulberry tree, over fences, across the creek and into the house. She was scratched and bleeding, one of her slippers gone.

Afterwards she was sick. "The lung fever again," the doctor said, but this time she mended quickly. It was summer. The man was thought to be from the poorhouse near Dodgeville, the last of the ex-slaves. When Kristin described him they knew this had been no *old* man. So the story took on dimension, until he became an escaped prisoner. That Fall, in school, she read *Uncle Tom's Cabin* and sorted the matter out for herself. The stranger must be a good man, she thought. That was her second lesson.

Later that Summer, there were a number of other occurrences, each stranger that the last. It could seem as if something greater than worldly presence was taking hold. The terror of this summer was captured through one such occurence, and she wrote of these things in the poem "A Summer Day That Changed The World."

In later days of her maturity, as a poet, it was pointed out to Kristin that if she were not psychic as a child, this poem nonetheless has a number of lines which indicated her to be. Had she made up the part about the dreams and the "bones turned black?" No, not made up. She had not even embroidered upon the actual event. Her seventh and eighth summer truly held never-to-be-forgotten experiences, unreal and frightening ones. To write of these effectively, without marring quality, their continuity in her narrative poems, some accounts had to be combined and simplified:

In mid-July on a Sunday afternoon, Kristin and Shep made a discovery. Father and Leo were at a town hall meeting, Mother, having taken her digitalis, was in siesta, snoring. Her dressing gown was clinging to her as if glued, for the humidity was high.

Kristin went out to sit in the north shade of the house. Kittens joined her, and soon Shep stood by, panting and casting jealous side-glances. Twice he whined and put his paw on her bare knee. "You want to go to the woods?" she asked. His tail fanned the air. Kristin got her sunbonnet and a paper bag to keep any flowers she might find from wilting. They were not going to the woods. She was wary of that so soon after seeing the black man.

The quarry was on an open hillside, a half-mile from the house. So far as Shep was concerned, a walk was a walk was a walk. On the way she picked flowers that grew only on their farm, tiny lavender cabbages, only they grew up and down a stalk like brussels sprouts. (Later in life she would lose a ten-year old son whose eyes were *lupine* lavender-blue.) There was pin-striped grass and minute star-flowers with scarlet centers. The wild asparagus plumes were already yellowing in the summer air.

Father thought some pioneers may have had a dwelling there, but Trapper Mose, who occupied a shanty-cabin half the year beside one of their ridge fields, had vetoed that assumption.

"Nope! Never white folk. Mebbe Injuns. A good lookout place, so I heard tell."

Shep went about his own excavations in the quarry while Kristin hunted for jewelled and colored rocks. Digging in dried moss, he was raising little puffs of lime dust. Then he started to bark, sharp, excited barks, before he stopped and looked toward Kristin.

She went to see. He had uncovered a set of bones. It was a foot, the bones in perfect order. She let out a little yell, thinking first of the black man. Oh no! These were white bones.

Then Father was right and Trapper Mose was wrong! But why find them now? The quarry was opened five years before. The whole basement of the new barn had been quarried here; she was told it was a gaping hole near the top of this steep hill, the size of several cellars. Until this moment it had seemed like having a playhouse-castle, of which she was the mistress. But the bones—when and how had they come?

A silence descended. Shep rubbed against her legs. The quietness all around seemed different, stillness itself. The tall trees on the horizon, the graybearded faces of boulders, the hill across the Valley, all stared at them. In the whole Valley, only stillness. She looked again. It was clearly and unmistakably a foot. They wasted no time getting home.

Mother and Leo laughed out loud at her report. Father looked interested, and said, "If it is a man's foot, it isn't going any place. Maybe I'll call John in the morning."

John was their neighbor and town chairman. Kristin knew she wasn't believed. That night, lying awake longer than usual, even the moon looked like it was laughing. She was dealing with mystery, with the unknown, and she had no directions. What do we know about *foreshadowings*, about childish terrors of darkness, lurking shadows and bones in quarries?

She got her rosary from the bedpost and began to say the *Aves* softly. Father came and knelt by her bed and responded with a few of the Holy Marys. "In the morning we will go to the quarry. Now go to sleep my little Kristin." He never called her that again.

In the morning they found the foot, and what went with

it. Father called Ole Paul and John and Doc Watson who was Justice of the Peace and a self-taught veterinarian. Archeologists could not have worked more carefully; when they were finished, they had a full-sized skeleton. It was white as milk.

The find was reported in three issues of *The Weekly Home News*, and the bones were kept at Doc Watson's place. When the fire at Taliesin came, the unknown skeleton was forgotten for awhile, but not by Kristin. Finally it was put into the ground in a plot where a few years later, Wild Rose O'Neill would be laid to rest.

There were always dreams; some of them recounted in the poem that was written about that Summer. In the real nightmares the bones were black and Kristin lay paralyzed in a woods where lady's-slippers bloomed. In happy dreams the skeleton was cast as Hiawatha, or John Alden, or as Ernest, who had come to look like THE GREAT STONE FACE. To the child Kristin, Wyoming Valley was the Mohawk Valley and New England not much farther off than Madison.

Today, some people are of the opinion that this poem should not have been written. Be that as it may. "A Summer Day That Changed the World" and "Young and Fair is Christopher" are the two most often requested at readings. I am indifferent as to opinions. The reliving of the traumatic experience was mostly unintentional, a burden that came unbidden.

About fifty years afterward, I was accompanying Richard Perrin around this historic area (the Uplands) in search of authentic old buildings that might be moved. He had in mind the creation of Old World Wisconsin.

The idea had come when he was in charge of rebuilding German cities after World War II. He had visited such outdoor museums in Scandinavia. That day we visited old churches, schools, homes and barns. Late afternoon we were at the Blue Grass Cheese Factory near House On The Rock and Fann's Hill. "We can't be very far from Taliesin?" he asked.

"I replied: "Two hills and about six miles," surprised that

he who had written so much about the architecture of Frank Lloyd Wright wanted to go there now. And, I ventured, "It's a good distance back to Milwaukee." (Mr. Perrin was its city planner at the time.)

"I have never seen Frank's grave. I need to see his resting place."

At the little cemetery, with its quaint, shingled-all-over chapel, we went first to the large fieldstone boulder that marked Mr. Wright's grave. Soon, as if from inner prompting, he hurried to another tombstone. He stood there in such somber study that, ill at ease, I finally joined him.

He was looking at an oblong, rounded stone, shaped like a shortened bolster pillow. In raised letters was spelled M-A--M-A-H.

"Frank fashioned this stone himself," he said. Then, after a pause, he asked, "Who, coming here, will have any idea who this woman was, what she meant to him?" It was more observation than question.

I took my time before saying, "Probably there are few still living who could tell you more about Mamah Borthwick than I."

And I told him of being there the day of the tragedy. He looked at me in startled silence. To break it, I said, "I should write a short story. So far it hasn't come."

"And it won't" he said. "Bernar McFadden was right: 'Truth is stranger than fiction.' No, you can't do it."

A day of hyperactivity: that night I was still awake at 3:00 A.M.; I slept and dreamed fitfully. Scenes came and went: I did not see Martha or my parents, or Leo or any of the people I knew were there that day, except for one, like a lone figure on a merry-go-round. The person was Andrew Porter, married to Mr. Wright's sister. They lived in a house nearby. Again and again he came toward me, tall and slim, his handsome countenance barely recognizable. The front of his white shirt was soaked with blood.

I awoke the next morning at the usual time. I came awake knowing that Richard Perrin was right: that experience could not be fictionalized. Maybe the only narrative it could be told in would be a poem. I knew that to do this I had to, as in the dream, get back into the mind of the child soon to be nine years old. I wrote the entire poem that day, though it underwent several revisions and restraints before it saw print.

I wrote a second ending. I did so from a mature viewpoint, guilt-ridden with my own neglects and transgressions, knowing I was willful and often a law unto myself, and having suffered devastating losses. This ending was compassionate, and as well-crafted as the first. There was not a hint of

> One man watching icicle-eyed
> while the other wept over rubble,
> raking with blistered hands in trickling smoke
> for bones eleven summers young—his son.

When I finished "A Summer Day That Changed the World" I realized that the onlooking man was probably suffering more than the boy's father. This was, in a sense, the replacement-child for his own sons whom he had deserted. Moreover, the boy was the son of the woman he loved so dearly.

When I was involved with the poem, I was regretting that I could have known Mr. Wright, my father's friend, fairly well. Because of that early impression out of prejudice, the privilege had been foregone.

What I have not regretted is that the second version was destroyed. Why? Because I might have been tempted to use it. It made me look better that I was. It also violated my credo as a poet.

In my years of teaching, every class heard a certain statement, my refutation of the idea of loose poetic license. A poem should be a testament: *this-is-who-I-am*: "Nothing weakens a poem so much as falsehood to the fact, either in one's emotions or the poetic vehicle that carries them."

The Box Social

Ben Cohen is saying "So you're ten now? Well, here's some candy for my best girl." In the white paper sack with green and red stripes are coconut bonbons in pretty pastels. He does not hear "Thank you, Mr. Cohen," because he is not really seeing Kristin, but looking at the tendrils of hair that curl almost into Mother's bodice. (She'd told Mother to wear her button-up blouse!)

"Your ladyfinger grapes are in the cooler," he says to her, "and we've plenty of winter pears. The chocolate pecan cookies are fresh. Just try one." There is much inspecting and decision-making before they are through with shopping. While two other women stand frowning, Ben takes the groceries and the brown and gold crepe paper to put into the tailgate of the buggy. Mother follows, carrying a box Ben has saved for her. Inside are the grapes and cookies and pears.

"See you at the box social," he says. Mother takes the lines from him, handing Kristin the box to hold.

On the way home she explains what to do if Father is there when they arrive: "Put your bonnet over the box and hurry upstairs to your room. We don't want him to see it."

Kristin's cheeks burn. She is angry, but afraid to show it. "Poor Father," she thinks, recalling how Ben (*and* the mailman *and* the cheese maker) looked at Mother and how he and the miller were always hurrying to help her. She has a sneezing spell and helps herself to another bonbon.

"You're forgetting your manners," Mother says, shaking her head when offered one. She adds, "Make them last. You don't want to be fat, do you?"

Father isn't there when they get home, so Mother takes the box into the root cellar while Kristin holds the horses' lines. She comes out with jars of canned beef and blackberries. "Good enough for us!" Kristin fumes to herself.

Just then Father drives in with a wagonload of corn. Sometimes Kristin cries for the horses, but not this time of year! It is their good time, pulling the wagon a few feet and then stopping while Father husks the rows of corn on both sides of the wagon as well as the row between the wheels. He does not ever have them reined, so they munch corn and leaves. For him it is back-breaking work.

As he drives up now, he looks so tired Kristin wants to run to him and say that she knows his hands and arms must hurt. It angers her the way Mother lets him carry the big grocery box into the house, never thanking him. She just smiles that soft smile, and he winks at her. She *does* say that she'll water the team, but Kristin knows she won't have to.

"No, Dear," Father says. "You get supper. I'm hungry as a wolf. I hope you got some fresh fruit. I'm getting sick of apples."

"Yes, bananas," she says, but not a word about Father's favorites, the grapes and the russet pears. Kristin wonders who is to have those. Not Ben, she knows, but someone Mother likes better than us.

After Kristin does the dishes, she washes her feet in the dishwater, rinses them with water from the rain barrel, and goes to bed, not because she's sleepy, but because she'd rather not kiss Mother good-night. Mother is still in the barn helping with the milking. Kristin looks at the moon and pretends to understand the night voices. Looking at mental pictures from the *Bible History for Children*, she falls into dark sleep to the distant screaming of roosters.

In the morning the two spring roosters are already lying on the kitchen table in pink and yellow pieces when she gets up. Mother has finished stiffening the bread sponge, water is boiling in the iron kettle. She drops in four small onions, some bay leaves and thyme, and the two breasts. She does not let the water quit boiling as she put in each piece.

"Like we did in Denmark," she explains, "for a good salad. For soup it doesn't matter. Now we will let it simmer."

She separates eggs. The whites will be for macaroons, the yolks, a mayonnaise for the chicken salad. Kristin stands on one foot, dripping olive oil into the yolks as Mother turns the new rotary beater. She thinks that when hurrying with her cooking, Mother is prettier than ever, like pink peonies in June. She begins to love her again.

"Will you get the scissors and the jar of flour paste we made yesterday?" Mother says. She already has the box and the crepe paper, the brown, the gold, and some pieces of green and white from another time, on the dining room table. "First we make gold chrysanthemums, three of them, and green leaves." She lays the box cover on the brown paper and cuts a piece exactly to fit. "Waste makes want," she says. Kristin cuts strips and flutes the edges to make a border on top so the flowers will seem to be in a natural setting.

"I hope it sells high. The social is to make money to buy a piano for your school," she says, admiring their creation. Some of her excitement takes hold of Kristin.

They have stewed chicken for dinner. Afterward Kristin bones the breasts and thighs and turns the meat grinder. Mother dices celery and hard-boiled eggs, and by unwrapping a dozen or more, finds two large and perfect tomatoes. She trims off the tops in a sawtooth pattern and then carefully scrapes out the insides. What chicken salad remains after making sandwiches, she mixes with peas and uses to fill the tomato shells.

Now the box. It is lined with two large linen napkins, lapped at the middle. Then all the foods, both plain and fancy, are arranged for color and size (a capsule-Danish smorgasbord). She decorates the box with celery-heart leaves and parsley from the pots on the window sill. "Oh," she says wistfully (this former sea-maiden), "A few shrimps would be so pretty. But they would smell!"

When the box is finished, it is wrapped in newspaper. "Your father mustn't see it. That's part of the fun."

"Fun!" she thinks angrily. "Fooling Father is fun?"

The evening comes as evenings will. The program at school goes well, but Kristin forgets two lines of her recitation of "Old Ironsides" and is doubly upset because she can see that nobody even noticed. Then she remembers the box and wishes she were brave enough to say something to the fellow who buys it.

Finally it is time. The table, covered till now with a sheet, and in back of the teacher's desk, is rolled forward on casters. The auctioneer whips off the covering and begins a low warm-up singsong of words. From the other side of the room, where the children must sit, Mother's box looks like a bowl of apricots on the cluttered table.

As Father walks past the table to join the menfolk, he touches with his big bony hand the corner of the chrysanthemum box. He turns a little and smiles at Mother across the room. Their look is like lightning, and Kristin shivers. Time lumbers on. Then the auctioneer is holding up their box, tilting it for all to see. A ripple passes through the crowd. The bidding *starts* at more than the last one sold for, and when the box is finally his, Father has paid six dollars. It is the last to be sold. When he opens it, several men gather round to see whose name is on the card. "Your own wife!" they say, as he sits down and motions Mother to come forward and join him. The grapes and pears he puts into the cover of the box, and everyone who comes to visit with them must have some. Kristin's plate lunch is good, but some of the beef sandwich sticks in her throat.

"Were they good?" Mother asks on the way home.

"Say! I never got any grapes," he says sheepishly.

"Oh, you knew very well I'd keep some at home for you," she says, and they both laugh. Even in the darkness Kristin feels awkward and in the way, and older than either of them. They drive on in silence and she wishes Leo was along and not riding with the neighbor boys.

Where they sleep, side by side, on these summer nights,

do they converse in that other silence? While grapes wilt on our counters, and battery-raised roosters go unprotesting to slaughter, are they saying:

"Remember, John, the chrysanthemum box?"

"Yes. It was beautiful as you, if that were possible."

It is too late for them to hear, from another room, the long-ago-child saying "I didn't know, Father, I didn't know it was for you."

Once at the Hour of Moonrise

During the winter of 1916, Kristin likened the weather to the Chimera in her favorite author's *The Wonder Book*. October through December was the goathead of that monster. Late September's killing frost opened on a month of rainy, sunless days which created a pall, the cold mounting continuously until the Holidays. She found it hard to think warmly of Pan, who was the other goat in her fanciful world. Then winter was upon them: the roaring blizzards, after which the moon and the stars glared from the domed cavern overhead. At times these inspired terror in Kristin's heart as truly as if a lion's head were at her big dormer window.

At last they were in a February thaw. The terrible serpent's head was reaching down out of the sky with its forked lightning tongue and foul breath. In the Valley there was talk of flu sickness again.

Since the last Bohemian peddler stopped by, four months had passed. Then one February day a stranger appeared. Unlike the others, who were always happy for being welcomed in an unfamiliar place, this one looked sullen and would not enter their kitchen. He refused the oven-fresh loaf of bread Mother offered him. Since Father was not home and the man was taciturn, they could not tell by his speech where he was from.

When he left the doorstep, they spoke of how thin he was and how his eyes had not met theirs.

He went directly to the spring as if he'd known it was there, where, staring into it a good while, he stooped to fill a canteen but did not drink. Instead, he pulled some watercress that was beginning to show, stood there and tore it apart, not looking at what he was doing, talking to himself.

That evening Kristin heard Father telling how the cattle did not go to their usual drinking spot a ways below the walled spring. They seemed wary, he said, and acted as if the stranger might be somewhere about. In a low voice he told Mother that the man had made a fire, earlier, after scarcely rubbing two dead pieces of wood together. "This was before he went to the house. I was watching him from the hill," Father said.

Kristin was always a listener. Perhaps it served her right that often she slept badly. This night, it seemed forever since the darkness began, which had never been more black. In place of the usual quiet, there was now a humming high above the Valley—like a motor heard from a distance. But the only machine thereabouts was Joe Julson's steam engine, used at threshing time. She thought it could be a big flock of birds returning early, and tried not to hear or to think about the cave with the man's bones, or the fire but two years past. Pleasant memories of good happenings would not come.

From the large room next to hers, there were comfortable snorings from the parental bed. She closed her eyes, wishing they did not always have to go to bed at nine o'clock. Finally she slept.

(Since that night it seems a century until I read Loren Eiseley's *Endure the Night*: "I have said that it is the sufferer from insomnia who knits the torn edges of men's dreams together in the hour before dawn. It is he from his hidden, winter vantage point who sees the desperate high-hearted bird fly through the doorway while the sleepy doorman nods. . . ." Since then I have understood my sufferings as a night person in that setting, at that time.)

Kristin wakened to the faintest light in the sky. Satisfied that the worst of the night was over, she lay staring out the window in that sleeping house. Soon she would make out the faint outline of the hill between their place, and the mill and the house Grandfather built, and which now belonged to Uncle Lew. The hill reminded her of a camel.

She was dozing off when Father jumped from his bed, muttering something in Bohemian. A towering woodsman, he seemed to be lifting a load that was either too heavy, or else it was fighting him. There was a hard scuffle. Though Kristin was frightened, she went to their door. His breath came in loud gasps as he put Mother, protesting, down in front of the bay window to the east. Pointing to the hill which showed quite plainly now against a chartreuse sky, he cried out: "See it there! A ball of fire going toward heaven!"

"Wake up John! You can't see the moon. It isn't up there."

"No, not the moon. A ball of fire, bigger than any moon."

Mother was strong and did not want for courage, but her words came trembling: "Please come back to bed. Please, John?" She struck a match to light the lamp.

Facing the window, he held a hand as if to shade his eyes from glare, then he turned to her. "You didn't see it, that blinding ball of fire?" There was such sorrow in his voice Kristin crept back to bed, shaking.

Mother said: "You are overtired from cutting cross-ties yesterday. Come now, dearest." She led him back to their bed.

For a short while he knelt in prayer and went then, she was sure, into Mother's arms. She cried silently, wishing it were her right to comfort him. Then she saw the first rays of a wintery sun peeking from behind the hump of the hill.

They were well along into new day when a messenger from his sister in Dodgeville brought the news that Baba (grandmother) had died. This was Mary Marish Kritz, who was born in May of 1832. Hours after Father's experience, he learned that his mother left this world that morning a little while before sunrise.

Today's children, they say, spend too much time watching television, that many of the fantasy films stultify rather than stimulate their imaginations. I do not know. I do see that some of these, and the cartoons, are patently a sales pitch to sell expensive toys.

This calls for decrial. Here I would say that I hope I never outgrow Yogi Bear, Bugs Bunny and such, or Sesame Street. I like the crustier Road Runner also. Violent? Children have always loved make-believe violence. It can relieve monotony or put overcharged minds on "hold."

When a child, I liked Poe's and Blake's poems, the perils of Ulysses, and Jehovah's awful vengeance. Especially enjoyable were the Milo Winter illustrations for Hawthorne's works. Neither was Dore too far-out for my taste. I think we have to trust the good sense of normal children. When the real and the more interesting happens along, they will want that. I did.

Valley Neighbors

"Old Uncle Eric"

In the studio loft that was to become the woman Kristin's brain, were many indiscerneable images and primitive figures like cave drawings. There have always been portraits crumpled to distortion, many erasures, and other pictures which may only be seen at certain times or in a special light.

The vignettes of "Uncle Eric" and "Martin L." as well as the story of Phileas, widely divergent characters, as they supplement Kristin's personal experiences, may serve as a microcosm of all the people who touched her life in that valley.

One such barely-chalked image was of everybody's Uncle Eric—*how* he re-emerged from Kristin's imagination. On a day very like the one in 1936, full of somber chill, overcast and very still, was December 14, 1942, the sixth anniversary of Kristin's son's death. The family had been driving and walking for several hours in the cemetery at Gettysburg. They were standing in front of the memorial to the First Minnesota Infantry, Eric's company. It was as if the thousands of slain men came at once into that space, their cumulative dread, grief and anguish enveloping her like a whirlwind. (Not too far in the future she could acknowledge that on anniversaries there was a strange association—a kind of repossession of her being by the departed.)

Kristin's teeth chattered, her breathing became shallow and she shook as if from ague. Only in the Rocky Mountains years later would such overwhelming emotion seize her. Two of the men in their small party came and put their arms around her closely for support. Only when they came to the car was she cognizant the men were her husband and the priest. Neither has the significance of this faded, nor has it been told until this writing. Questioned, she said, "It was old Uncle Eric."

To further questions, she could only answer, "I don't remember. I'll have to turn over a lot of pages in my mind."

Every summer Uncle Eric came from Faribault, where he lived in a kind of Old Soldiers' Home, to stay with his nephew and sole relative, Ole Paul. Several times each summer he paid visits to them. As he was very old, frail, and deaf, how he managed the half-mile walk was a marvel in itself, when at first, he came alone. (Later years, Earl or Laurence, or both, would accompany him. Then Leo and the boys would run outside, saying there were chores to do and leaving Mother to cope. Eric simply came and sat.)

His conversation was the same each year, telling how he'd lost his hearing at Gettysburg. The shell had taken the head right off the soldier next to him: "I was splattered all over with his blood. I couldn't hear anymore. Oh, but we closed ranks." How many times of an afternoon he'd repeat that—"Oh but we closed ranks!"

Mother once said it was more than twenty. But she was very patient, serving him coffee with whatever sweets were on hand, getting out her mending or crocheting, smiling and nodding her head. (She owed Ole and Jane Ann and Bertha and Ernie, and she was ever-conscious of such debts). Kristin, pretending she was reading, sat and listened.

Sometimes, Eric sat and seemed to be pondering. Or else looking at Mother, he spoke of the War, his words becoming garbled while he stuttered badly. Mother would get up and put a cookie in his hand, or pat his back, glaring at Kristin, who was giggling herself into a case of hiccups. Speaking of the battle, Eric always ended with the same phrase, stuttering, "We w-w-were b-b-busy a-a-as a-a-a d-d-dog w-w-with f-f-fleas."

Over and over and over. . . .

Uncle Eric was living history, wasted on Kristin, who deserved his haunting.

"Martin L."

Martin, too, had a stock phrase. "Mun dun, mun dun, mun dun" he'd say, shaking his head when he'd been drinking and had to be looked after. He was not living history, but an ordinary, illiterate neighbor. Kristin remembers him chiefly because he was a symbol of the care the folk of upper Wyoming Valley had for each other.

Martin and Minnie lived at the uppermost tip of the Valley in what should be described as a cove, the best location possible for their poor little house. Two rooms were constructed of logs and there was a lean-to of rough boards. The floors were earthen, spread in winter with a thick layer of marsh grass which Martin scythed near the river and hauled home. Their forty acres were mostly hill and brush, submarginal for all but about ten; the high hills protected three sides of the house and there was a thick growth of cedars to the west.

They had five children. Four were grown and gone when Kristin was there. Only Annie, two years older than Leo, was still at home, which meant she was born the year Mother and Father came from Chicago, and was probably why Kristin never heard them calling her a "catch colt" or a "woods colt."

How many trips Kristin made astride her horse, old Beauty, was anybody's guess, for Mother disliked seeing "things go to waste!" Asparagus, rhubarb, apples, pickling pears and sweet corn were excuses to visit Annie.

Minnie seemed almost as old as Baba, so brown and wrinkled. She smoked and sat dozing in her chair, but when Kristin was ready to leave, she would pick a bouquet of flowers for Mother, who receiving them, invariably remarked, "Anyone who can grow such beautiful flowers should have a better garden."

Martin was usually off hunting, fishing or trapping, or killing rattlers for their bounty. He had a nice sense of reciprocity; our family enjoyed plump rabbits or, from time to time, a couple of squirrels we would not otherwise have had. Father would have no guns or traps on the place.

One day, or night, Minnie simply slept away, and within a year Annie left home and went to Madison to find work. Kristin's last errand up that road was to take Martin a fresh loaf of bread and an apple pie. Martin was drinking more those days. When Kristin was on Beauty's back, ready to leave, he asked her to wait; he went into the house and brought out two big plants, an English ivy and a jade, each growing in a worn-out milking pail. He put a handle in each of her hands and gave Beauty a slap on the rump, saying, with a wave of his hand toward the encircling hills, already bare of most of their autumn splendor: "Tell your Maw they'll freeze here."

The mare ambled home, sure-footed, and Mother was so thrilled with the fine plants that Kristin didn't mind that her arms felt two inches longer. (Mother still had the ivy, transplanted many times, which was started on its second encircling along the picture molding of the dining room when, in 1954, she too simply slept away.)

Martin became a regular caller, bringing his few letters to be read to him. Three times there were letters from Norway announcing the demise of relatives. Mother could read these fairly well since the written languages are quite similar.

When he was "under the weather" he would come and ask Mother, "Kristina, you could make me some sweet soup, mebbe?" This was sago cooked with brown sugar, cinnamon bark and raisins, served with cream. Mother surmised his sickness was from being alone, for in those days the sago had first to be soaked in cold water, which took, in all, a couple of hours. Not that he didn't enjoy, slurping and making low, contented grunts. They all enjoyed, for Mother had made sweet soup enough for the family.

Then there were his all-day trips to Spring Green. Mornings the skin-and-bones sorrel team (part broncos he got from a peddler) went by with heads drooping, Martin sitting very straight in his light wagon. Often, at dusk, they were heard before seen, coming on a gallop around the nearest bend like a pair of colts.

If the weather was cold and Martin nowhere in sight, Ben Benoy, John Mainwaring or Father were on the telephone. (Ole Paul lived back a way on a private road, though once in awhile Ernie was called on to "go look.") One of the first things said was "Is it your turn, or is it mine?" The upshot was that someone (mostly Father since he lived nearest) would investigate if Martin had in fact been stretched out in the wagon box. Summers they did not bother about this overly, but when the weather was inclement they saw to getting him into the house, a fire built, the horses unhitched and turned loose.

These were the times when Martin mumbled, "Mun dun, mun dun, mun dun" till stupor again overcame him. The men took this to be a version of Norwegian "thank you," and now and then, among themselves, they called him, good-naturedly, "Ol' Mun Dun." But if any of them ever complained about Martin, it was not heard by Kristin.

Then she went away to school and Martin L. joined a growing line of those pilgrims who enter the caves of memory and are soon forgotten. (Now, since I am never one to devise ways to be rid of shadows, these people in the floor silt beg to be remembered.) There was Doc Watson the self-taught veterinarian, who, taking the second or third piece, would say to Mother: "Man is a pie-eating animal!"; Billie Davies who was constantly offering the Valley ladies rides in his fancy buggy behind an outrageously flatulent gelding; Louis Duvall who drove mules and claimed he could read the stars. (There were others. Many. In the excavation of a life, one should be selective. The question to be answered is, *why these two*?)

The answer may lie in a look at any day's obituaries that list a child or a young person. Often astounding is the number of surviving grandparents, sometimes four full sets plus even more great-grandparents, offshoots of divorces and remarriages.

Kristin recalls her situation. There was only Baba, born in 1832, nearing 80 when Kristin can form a mental image of her. She spoke only Bohemian and communication was nil. Hers had been an incredibly hard life; she was emaciated, bald, toothless, and partially blind. Being so, she clutched, rather than embraced, movements apt to fright a child, fear difficult to outgrow. There was no grandfather. There was Uncle Lew, the eldest of Father's brothers, memorialized in poems.

Which leaves "Uncle Eric," four months of every year. And there was "Martin L." Each of them filled an esoteric void in Kristin's life.

Phileas Comes to the Valley

"He's part Indian!" the grown-ups said in much the same way they might have said, "He's part timber wolf." Kristin puzzled over this. Indians weren't a novelty. He did not look fierce. His face was no darker, his cheekbones no higher than her Bohemian uncles. His nose was like Father's, which was said to be "Roman."

Phileas came as an innovation to Wyoming Valley. That is stating the incidence of his arrival charitably. Within a year or so some neighbors swore he was loco. They said it cautiously because of his father, and because his grandfather was the first settler in the Valley.

His father, Ben Wysuphberg, was their town chairman. Ben was a fine-looking, senatorial type, Prussian, and given to explosive opinions. So it was up to fifteen-year-old Leo to explain to her that Phileas' Indian blood was not the issue, but that Ben had sired him. All this surfaced when Ben's heart gave out and he had to quit farming. That is when Phileas, whom no one except Father seemed to have known about, was summoned. They lived on adjoining farms.

At the time of his heart attack, Ben had a second wife and two daughters. The youngest was Kristin's age, ten, and they were good friends. It seemed that in his late teens, Ben had left the Valley for the Dakotas and was gone for five years. That is all that the Valley folk knew about his young manhood. When he returned, he married, within a year, Alice, a young woman from across the river. Now, suddenly, there was Phileas. Ben, who answered to no one, explained that he had married an Algonquian and that this was the son of that union. That and nothing more did he ever tell.

Phileas arrived in Wyoming Valley on March 1st 1916, having written his father that he was bringing his own livestock. Therefore, Ben sold his cattle and a young team of horses before moving into town. He was good with figures and had been promised work in the courthouse. There would be rent from the land, the machinery and from the old team. Alice was a accomplished seamstress; they would manage.

Things would prove to be not so simple for the family. Life was difficult on these early farms. (Reading the ubiquitous reminiscences in today's publications for older readers, I am struck by a kind of black-out on what had to be one of the most challenging endeavors of those yesteryears: how did the farmer make a living in the wintertime so as to not have used up his savings before spring planting? Most of these nostalgic accounts are relatively straight-forward, and begin "*we would . . .*" One then reads about the way it was in the towns, at schools and churches, at the mills and in the homes. What about the ice-locked land of our northern states? What about the barns? No milking parlors, no insulation or heated outbuildings? Feed was often in short supply as was fodder for bedding. And "snow-bound" did not necessarily mean Whittier's poem.)

These were some of the problems Phileas was to encounter. He brought to the Valley his wife, Annie, and two young children, Helen and Austin. His "livestock" consisted of four airedale dogs: a male named Cobb and three bitches, Ol' Susannah, Jolie and Meta. There were also four ferrets, a pair of cats and a short-lived bronco. Phileas' plan was to raise dogs and ferrets for the surrounding communities. The dogs would protect and lighten the workload for the farm family. The ferrets were to keep the building free of rodents. And Siamese kittens could add a little class and status to an otherwise drab household.

The second summer and autumn, there were from time to time twenty or more hungry airedales running loose and howling along the creek and through the woods. These dogs gave a lifetime value as to the relativity of things; ever afterward, one vocal dog seemed small cause for a nuisance complaint.

Kristin liked the cats but they were not hardy as outdoor animals. The ferrets were more unpopular. These strange creatures could so lengthen their bodies that if directed into a No. 2 lamp chimney, they would turn around and meet their tails coming out. The rural folk preferred the rodents over bloodthirsty ferrets.

And the people of the Valley liked to hunt their own game. There was no police work for the terrier airedales. More than that, the game having been decimated, when a sheep or a calf was mysteriously killed and eaten, the suspect dogs had to go.

The third spring Phileas sent away to a mail order company and began a beekeeping operation. In that rich and flowering Valley, honey bees should have done well; there should have been plum and cherry and apple blossoms for the honey, as well as clover and millet and various wildflowers. The swarms he ordered soon got a disease known as "foul brood" and all were winter-killed or else sickened in other ways.

There came a gradual and subtle change in the way people reacted to Phileas. He was likable and neighbors began making excuses for him. They said he was "an idea and a theory man" and that he liked research. They also said, "Phileas is a little lazy; it's the Indian in him." What they had no explanation for, was how Phileas managed to finagle loans. About that, they made such remarks as, "That fellow could sell matches in hell." This was before the gag about selling refrigerators to Eskimos.

His enterprise for the next growing season was peanuts. The topic of many conversations was then how he had gotten a tight-fisted cattle dealer to finance the project. "Birds of a feather!" some said, for farmers are often suspicious of cattle-buyers.

Ben's farm was all bottom-land, a heavy clay. That summer, the rains hardly ever stopped, and when it did, the sun shone fiercely. The result was a baked topsoil, which would have been better suited to a potter's wheel than for growing peanuts. The flower stalks could not push into the ground to form the pods. Crop failure!

This went on for nearly seven years, bringing Phileas' experimental farming full circle—back to where Ben had left off. The son announced that he was getting into dairying for winter production, starting off modestly with nine cows which would freshen in November and December. Neighbors were somewhat heartened; they advised him to bank the sides of the old barn with soil, manure and straw, which in spring could be hauled onto the fields. They told him to nail oiled feedbags over the windows and to fill all chinks with clay.

None of which he heeded. Realities of farming here did not set well with Phileas. He had come from North Dakota where, he said, "the snow is insulation enough." Also he told them that they, the old-line farmers, had been foolish to be doing their milking in the hot months when their product was hard to keep. "And," he said, "it should be done in winter, not when crop-raising was in full swing." Kristin had always felt an affinity for Phileas, and this time she wondered if they had not been a bit stupid not to have figured this out for themselves.

It was an open winter. January brought temperatures twenty to thirty degrees below zero almost every night. The other cows in the Valley were dry of milk, their udders contracting close up to warm bellies, where gestation for spring calving was in process. Phileas' unfortunate beasts were full-teated and low-hanging, tender and moist from twice-daily milkings. The udders froze nearly solid.

Father, another neighbor and Phileas tried to save them. Those painful details need not be described. It was well that no Society For the Prevention of Cruelty to Animals had been organized, or this time he might have been in trouble. The cows were marked at a considerable loss. Furthermore, there were confrontations between Ben and his tenant-son. Father said, "It's a miracle that Ben didn't have another and fatal heart attack!"

On March 1st in those years, farm-moving day, Phileas moved his family, now numbering five, to an adjacent fruit farm.

Eventually he talked the owner into building an unusual combination root-cellar and forage loft.

Then his interest in the fruit business waned. It should be said that this was not wholly his fault. Almost every family, town and country, now had an orchard or a small variety of such trees. People have described similar situations clearly when they say that *not money but the lack of money is the root of evil.* Annie took the children and went back to Dakota to live with her mother.

Phileas hung on for awhile. He began planting ginseng, but it is a long-term venture, taking several years before any kind of harvest. (Later others would profit from this crop.) Phileas then took to tanning hides, which was not very lucrative. "A pity he did not find his niche sooner," Father said. "He's an artist! No one ever turned out softer or more beautiful leather."

Quite often Phileas helped out on our farm, where winter income was from supplying railroad ties for the market at Lone Rock. Again he merited Father's praise: "I've never had anyone as good at spotting the best white oak, or at hand-hewing the logs into prime ties."

These times he lived with us and we got to know him. Kristin learned how he had acquired his unusual name: a medical missioner had assisted at his birth on the reservation and baptized him "Phileas." Later he gave the young mother his copy of Jules Verne's *Around the World in Eighty Days*. Phileas had a few years in the mission school and he really identified with the hero of his favorite book, Phileas Fogg. There was speculation at times how much this had to do with his lack of practical sense.

But he tired of the hard physical labor with Father, and left us to move into an abandoned shack near town. He truly became an Ishmael; people began avoiding him, he became vocal on social issues and wrote long involved letters to newspapers. He also "got religion" and was an evangel who would hold forth for any listener.

Inexorably, days, weeks, months moved on as Phileas went his lonely way. Meanwhile, the regular country folk went their separate ways, engaged in more than mending harness, cracking nuts and making babies. For none of such activities put money into the Mason fruit jar or the local bank. None of those who wrested a livelihood from the soil during the first third of this century, then as in the present day, could ignore the necessities: some foods had to be bought, children and horses had to be shod. There were taxes and medical bills and amenities. Money vanished as fast as it does today.

Finally, Kristin's own family was grown and gone, and there was time for some real community service. But she will not forget the day she came upon Phileas in the County Home. He was so little-changed in appearance she could scarcely believe it. His distinctively handsome face was wrinkled and the dark auburn hair greying; the strange brown eyes still held that peculiar light that had intrigued her as a child. He was slim and straight and walked like a dancer. His gentle voice was the same, his quiet manner unchanged. Kristin was unable to describe her shock at finding his memory of life in the Valley totally gone.

The time for being kind to Phileas was brief: about two years after she chanced upon him, nearing the twilight hour during a February blizzard, he wandered away from the home. Next morning he was found sitting cross-legged against a boulder, Indian that he was, facing East. Probably because his was a country burial, the mortician had used no cosmetics. For that Kristin was grateful and for the slightly off-center half-smile that she would always associate with him. Hers were his only flowers and these, she insisted, go into the pine casket with him.

Kristin was never able to sort out his life. Had he been born into a century too soon, or too late? Under other circumstances might he have been an inventor, an artist, or a writer? There had been an extraordinariness about him that with strangers soured from lack of understanding. True, he was odd and imperfect. However, in today's economy of loose loans and grants; in a climate of heightened self-expression, respect for creativity and too-frequent acclaim for mediocrity, and of exploitation, might Phileas have flourished? Or would he have lost touch with physical reality even sooner? All of these she recognized as happenstances to be let go. . . .

One incident, however, will not go away: As Kristin was about to leave his nursing home room that last time, Phileas gestured that she tarry a moment. From under his bed he got out an old valise in which were a number of worn road maps, some random charts and hand-drawings. "We are planning a voyage," he said, "but it all depends on whether we can convince the Queen to furnish us with ships."

"How many ships do you need? And who do you mean, *we?*" she asked.

"We must have four—my co-captain, Columbus, and I." He lapsed into dreamy silence. "You'll hear of us!" he said prophetically.

The Years Slipped Away to the Rear

Spring came early to the Valley that last summer of Kristin's childhood there—years of development, which often seemed like "internment." Because of the early Spring, all crops were accelerated. Mid-June the oats were turning gold, which meant that the family had to get the loose mowed hay into the barns before readying the binder. Always the canvasses had to be repaired because of rodents. No farmer has ever figured why haying weather has to be insect-ridden, hot and humid. They can, with good reason, only complain.

Kristin would never ride on the heaped-high loads coming down the hill from the ridge fields. It was a rough walk and a needless foolishness, as Leo pointed out. He stretched out on top of the swaying mass and, resting, enjoyed the ride. Maybe it was the gambler in him, the fatalist, she guessed. But it was a dangerous road, carved into a steep side hill with several sheer drops on the opposite edge.

She would have gladly stayed on the ridge the whole afternoon, but she was needed to lead the old mare on the hayfork lift. When she came to the huge cottonwood tree that grew in the ditch so far below that its top was scarcely above the roadbed, she saw an immense bull snake reclining on a branch. It so startled her that she felt sick to her stomach.

She did not feel good. It was nothing that could be described, but simply a malaise. Soon she would know the word for it: *unwell.* Why it would be ever an offensive word is still not clear to her. As unlikely then as walking on the moon were today's advertised venalities on the relative merits of pads, or the douche-peddlers vying for poetic trade-names for vinegar and water.

Walking down that steep, rocky road in back of the mammoth load of fragrant clover, which only the young draft horses could hold back, she now felt apprehensive. Her legs seemed to be sticking together. A kind of wetness was there.

Raising her dress a bit, she saw the blood, wished she could die. ("Next load I'll ride down the hill and God will let the wagon tip over!") Even believing such thoughts to be sinful, she meant it. She knew nothing of pre-menstrual blues, except from what she had observed. Mother was usually cross at these times and twice had said, "You'll find out!" Then, later, "You'll know when it's time."

Unreal? Incredible? Kristin had no girl companion, none her own age. When she was in the under-grades all the girls were older. Now, and for three years past, she was often the only student at school. There were children in first, second, fourth and fifth grades who did not often come during the hard winter months. Teacher was a cranky spinster who on occasion whacked her with whatever book was at hand. This was a "religious" woman who, when they were alone, insisted they top off the day's enlightenments with a recitation of the rosary. Kristin had never had a girl-to-girl talk.

Painfully modest, she had once, when going to town, wrapped a long scarf over her budding breasts, until Mother saw the safety pins. Now she thought to run on ahead to the creek below the barn and tidy herself. But when she came alongside the horses, and the house was in view, there was a big, black car parked between the root cellar and the summer kitchen. It must be Charlie's Reo! Cousin Marie and her husband had arrived from St. Paul earlier than expected. Kristin liked Marie very much.

Mother had never gotten over disciplines learned at the

Shepards. She hated having guests arrive before they were expected. Kristin forgot her own plight and worried that Mother might show her displeasure.

When they came to a stop at the bottom of the hill, Father said, "Leo and I will unload. Go in the house, dear, and make yourself pretty, or Marie will scold me for working you so hard."

Kristin sneaked into the summer kitchen and took a quick "sponge bath" at the sink there. Charlie came out the back door of the house and walked slowly to the upper driveway of the barn. She was relieved not to have to meet him now, surprised that he looked older than Father. She went into the house so quietly the women did not hear her. All seemed well.

Marie was more like a sister than a niece. She was the daughter of Father's eldest sister who had died giving her birth. *Baba* (which is "grandmother" in Bohemian) had raised Marie along with Henry, her own youngest and last child. When the orphaned baby came, Father was eight or less. Marie was overly fond of Kristin, Mother said, and the relatives were wrong when they said the two looked alike. "Same dimples, wide brow, sparkly eyes," they said. Kristin hoped it was true, but Mother said "No! You're like my sister in Denmark."

Marie held out her arms. "Such circles under your eyes, child!" she said. "And you are thin!" (Thin was not then synonymous with beauty.) Marie looked for Mother to say something and when she didn't, went on: "You're not happy, are you dear?"

Marie, perfumed, in silk *crepe de chine*, embraced her, and Kristin, who almost never wept, began to cry for no reason. Mother was openly shocked. Marie was enjoying her role as Comforter, and Kristin, newly a stranger to her own body, needed her comfort. When Marie released her and stepped back, there were bright splashes of blood on the bleached maple floor.

"You've got the Curse!" she said. "You're one of us now!"

"The Curse?"

"Yes, darling, that's what we call it. This means you are a real woman now, not a girl anymore!"

"Really, Marie, I never heard the like!" Mother said.

"If you say so," Marie sassed, squinting, compressing her

cupid's-bow lips. "Come dear, I've a belt and napkins. We'll fix you up. And clue you in on what all this *is*.

Charlie was a man of the world, well-dressed and friendly. Father and Kristin liked him. Leo thought he was "slick," whatever that meant. This was supposed to have been a honeymoon visit of sorts. They planned to stay a week but they left on the morning of the fifth day. "Charlie is bored," Marie said, "he's never been on a farm before." But Kristin knew there were other reasons, several of them.

A couple of years past, after one of Marie's visits, Kristin had overhead Uncle Paul explaining her to Mother: "Marie was about fourteen when John went to Chicago. She was inconsolable for months. We all knew how much she loved him and you may as well understand that too." After that, Kristin noticed how Mother was uneasy when Marie sat close to Father and made signs of affection.

Since the last Easter, there was an added reason for Mother's disapproval of Marie. Another cousin, Elizabeth, also living in St. Paul, was an elementary school teacher who had gone there on Marie's invitation. But soon, Elizabeth was aware of Marie's lifestyle and disassociated herself. Elizabeth was a large, ruddy-faced young woman who had, according to Father, "an inflated opinion of herself, and a tongue hung in the middle."

Since her mother's death, Elizabeth visited various uncles and aunts for vacations, always at Easter to Uncle John's. She had a married sister living on Pleasant Ridge where the work was heavy and the children too numerous for her to spend much time. This summer, Elizabeth was getting extra schooling in Minneapolis.

Last Easter, in conversations on the evenings when she and Mother sat at the dining room table, knitting or doing embroidery, she was full of bad news about Marie. Father was usually in the warm sun porch reading the paper. Kristin knew he could hear them gossiping, and that she could also hear, that she was not asleep in the room above, with its floor register. He never shielded her from this kind of knowing.

So now she listened. It seemed that Marie had always been a loose woman. She'd heard that before, several times. Marie, it would seem, had met Charlie, a wealthy cigar manufacturer and a married man with the youngest of his sons already at the University.

"Last I heard, his wife was dying," Elizabeth said. "In fact I think she has died. Marie has notions he'll marry her, but don't you believe it!"

"Why wouldn't he marry her in time?" Mother asked.

"Men never marry those kind! Besides, why spoil a good bargain?" Elizabeth laughed loudly. There was more gossip.

So here they were in the house three months later, Marie and Charlie, Mother not even sure they were married, Father not caring whether they were or not. Kristin was soon to discover that bottled-up anger is a time-bomb; the event marked the end of her eavesdropping for awhile.

One day, the four were in the parlor. Mother was showing Charlie the album with the photos of herself looking like Queen Marie of Roumania.

"Taken on shipboard," she said, "by an American correspondent on his way home from China. He fell in love with me."

"What went wrong?" Charlie asked. (To the others, it was an oft-told tale.)

"I was a married woman," Mother said primly.

"Oh, I supposed this was when you were coming to America."

"No, this was when I went back to Denmark when my father was very ill."

"Without your husband? Without John!" Marie said wickedly, now being her turn. "A beautiful girl has to be watchful of her powers."

"Well I certainly did nothing to encourage him!" Mother said.

Marie laughed. "Oh bosh! Tell that to the birds, or be honest."

Again Mother protested, and Father said something supportive.

"All right, play innocent then," Marie said, "but I don't mind telling you that when I wanted to, I could attract any man. Yes, even across a crowded room. And I wanted to, plenty of times."

There was soft laughter from Charlie and Father.

Mother said: "And I suppose you are proud of that? Bragging about it! You . . . Chippie!"

There was a hard, long silence, then Marie said, "Better mind your words, lady. That girl of yours is going to have that same power. Will you be able to stop her, keep her hidden away?"

Then the fireworks really began. Kristin tried not to hear. This was what becoming a "real girl" meant?

When they left next morning, Marie held Kristin close for awhile. "Oh honey, how I wish you were mine," she whispered. When she got into the car, she was tearful.

For the next two weeks, Kristin wanted to write to Marie and tell her how sorry she was about the things Mother had said —and that Father had not interfered on her behalf. What good to write if she couldn't say what she meant? Mother always read her letters to make sure there were no mistakes.

Kristin forgot about writing until later. Then came the letter that resolved the whole thing. It was from Sacred Heart Academy, Edgewood Villa, Madison, Wisconsin, addressed to Mr. and Mrs. John Kritz. It said that the Sisters of Saint Dominic would welcome their daughter to the Academy, that although the notice was short, an exception was being made because Father Brudermanns had recommended her highly. However, the letter explained, there was a six-weeks probation. School was to begin in five weeks. There was enclosed an application form and a printed list of the articles of clothing and other items she was to bring.

No one consulted with Kristin as to whether or not she wanted to go away to school. She had taken for granted she would attend high school in Spring Green, boarding in someone's home and coming back to the Valley every Friday. There were young folk in town, girls and boys that she had looked forward to knowing. She was not astute enough to associate this development with the quarrel between Mother and Marie. It seemed likely to have more to do with brother Leo's experiences.

He stayed at the Wells Hotel, as did several other country boys. The first two years he had excellent grades, always a few "A"s, which was most commendable for one from a rural school. Then something changed, until in the second semester of his third year, he was bringing home "C"s and an occasional "F". Professor Rohr, the principal, suggested a physical examination. "The boy is falling asleep in classes," he said. Before it came to that, one of the other boys snitched.

Spring Green was a railroad town. There were cars for rent, and a good livery stable. The Wells Hotel was a mecca for salesmen. Time hangs heavy on men away from home and card playing was a favorite pastime.

Leo, like Mother, was a natural at cards. He was large for his age and a daily shaver, so it was a shock to many of the salesmen that their nightly poker-playing companion was only sixteen-or-so years old. He was a formidable opponent—even in his younger days.

Later he would become quite well-known on that circuit. He was called "Cap" (for Captain). How he acquired the nickname was never known. He was smart and clever and managed very well. When he married and "settled down" at thirty, doubtless those years of mental agility served him well. Leo was prosperous.

Mid-August: the last Sunday Mass at the parish church! Next Sunday the family would go to Dodgeville to say goodbye to Aunt Annie and other relatives. Going away to boarding school was an event. Today Kristin felt very alone, bouncing about in the backseat of the big Buick.

It was nicer when Leo was along—he and Father in the front seat, she and Mother in the back. Leo was eighteen, since March, and asserting himself, having a life of his own. Last night

Hank Larson had picked him up, enroute to Mineral Point, then Dubuque on Sunday. "Cards and gambling, I suppose?" Mother had said sourly. Leo only smiled and said, "Maybe." But he had promised Kristin he would be in Dodgeville for the next Sunday.

She sat now in the big pew, eighth row from the front, listening with all her senses, heart beating in her throat. It had not been like this for a long time, not since she was much younger and had brought flowers for the altars. Usually she was distracted by the people, especially by children her own age. There was Pauline, the banker's daughter, home from school summers, who wore fine clothes and always seemed to stand on one foot with the toe of her other slipper just touching the floor. It was so graceful, Kristin thought, and now I'll be going away to school. She glanced at Mother on her left, Father on her right, both so straight and nice looking, and she felt insignificant. She didn't know *why* today was different.

When Father Brudermanns sang the *Pater Noster*, she remembered a parish celebration when an older priest had reminisced, during the banquet, telling how in 1902, when Bishop Frederick Katzer had appointed Father Brudermanns the official Chanter for the Milwaukee Archdiocese, he had said: "Among all the brethren, this is the richest voice, and I don't mean only in the clergy."

It was as if a bright light shone on everything. Then, when Christina Blau sang *Panis Angelicus*, a deep sadness overcame her that she only vaguely comprehended the next summer when Chistina was "laid to rest." She was seventeen and had diabetes before there was supplemental insulin.

The Blessed Virgin's statue directly in front smiled down on them and the snake under her foot did not matter. Not today. The main altar, as well as this side altar, had extra candelabra, for it was not only a Sunday, but the Feast of the Virgin's Assumption into heaven as well.

Kristin banished from her mind all thought of that fire, five years past, this very day. A picture of Martha flashed through her mind and she offered a prayer of contrition. There was more than sadness attending Kristin. God was back in the church, as He had not been (for her) for a good while. He hovered in sunlight streaming through stained glass windows and when Christina's long solo ended and the Communion bells were rung, the air was crowded with invisible angels.

Outside, on the way to the car, she saw arrows of birds above the distant fields. Fall was hurrying in over the broad valley and its surrounding hills and bluffs. Only the fast-moving, treacherous River would fail to acknowledge that.

As on every Sunday after Mass, they went directly to the Wells Hotel for dinner. This practice was uncommon among the Valley folk. It was Father's thank you to Mother for feeding us so well all week.

Today Kristin was not joyous, as usual, anticipating the delicious meal. "No smile for me today?" Mrs. Lute Wells asked, ushering them to a window table. To Mother she said, "We've a special dessert! It's pecan pie and if you like, I'll give you the recipe."

Kristin knew this was in exchange for Mother's generous sharing of recipes. Oh, it was even better than lemon pie or sour cream raisin, she thought, and when Mother said this was the case to Mrs. Wells, she did not feel disloyal.

The next Sunday was memorable mainly for small gifts. Father Ambauen gave her his latest book, *Winged Words*, in which she later found the words from *King Solomon* on "Vanity" he'd said at her baptism. That day, when she noted the publication date was 1921, he explained: "It's an advance copy. It will not be distributed until spring—for Easter."

Then came the leave-taking day. Father dropped her off at the rectory while he and Mother went shopping. Father Brudermanns would bring her to the depot where they'd all say goodbye. He too had books for her, ones she'd cherish all her life: *Poems by Gerard Manley Hopkins* (with notes by Robert Bridges) and Oscar Wilde's *The Ballad of Reading Gaol*—an exquisitely printed copy, bound in softest suede.

And one other, over which he chuckled, giving it to her. It was a *Life of Service, Memoir and Poems* of Rev. John Durward. Father Brudermanns said, "We were standing in the raw March wind at Durward's Glen, while admiring friends read extensively from his poems. Archbishop Messmer muttered, 'They should have buried his verses with him.' " Through the Father, she already knew there was a difference between poetasters and real poets.

On the train she opened the Durward book and the first line she saw was: "The years slipped away to the rear." For a brief bit of time she was not dry-eyed.

Thus, during the last week of August 1920, Kristin went neither blithely nor apprehensively off to the city to school. She was still docile and accepting, unsure whether this was a reward or not, and paying little heed to the realities. The "Roaring Twenties," like the "Gay Nineties," about which Mother and Father knew plenty, having spent those years in Chicago, were opening on a new era of Wickedness. Or so 'twas said.

Kristin would have growing-up children of her own before she fully understood the cost to themselves of those early advantages. The times were good, but not necessarily for farmers, and tuition was high, for it included bed and board. Going away, Kristin knew that Mother would miss her help.

Soon she would appreciate the boxes of cookies and fudge and the special-occasion clothes—all incidentals to the real sacrifice. Across the fence from the farm buildings were sixty acres of rich bottomland belonging to Owen King. Father had been wanting to convert the rough ridge fields to more utilitarian crops such as winter rye and wheat and herd's-grass, thus eleminating the long, too frequent, trips to the barn. They had planned to buy the land that fall but did not do so until her schooling ended.

But such appreciation is generally a late-blooming annual, one that grows more abundantly with age. Thus wiseacres point out, periodically, that there is no training for parenting, one of live's most important and demanding careers.

How can there be such? The sets of rules change with every situation, with each individual. (Yes, there are some basic rules.) And that's the holy rub—the problems. And who is to conduct these training courses? Doubtless, the childless.

The majority of parents love their children. Rearing a family has to be day-to-day, one-on-one confrontations, decisions, compromise, when those adorable babies and pre-schoolers arrive at the age of self-assertiveness. Then later, when they become parents, they may realize that being a psychology major might avail them nothing.

Which leaves us all with the hope that memories of the good, the happy, the just, may outweigh those that are bitter or painful. That seems to be the pattern of life as played out by fallible humans—not robots. And so "the years slip away to the rear."

Edgewood Years

Kristin arrived from Wyoming Valley wearing high-laced shoes and with her hair, usually in braids, flying loose. Later, classmates enjoyed telling what a "hick" or "hayseed" she seemed. The time was a few weeks before her fourteenth birthday, late August 1920.

The girl's boarding school was called Sacred Heart Academy by the Dominican Sisters, whose property it was at that time. Early in Wisconsin statehood, the huge mansion had been built as the home of Governor Washburn, and was called Edgewood Villa. It is now the site of Edgewood High School and College.

The Academy had a dress code, and Mother, educated in the strict manner of Danish Lutherans, took the instructions literally. The gym-suit was especially notable. It was to be made of black sateen, below-the-knee bloomers with twenty-six pleats. With this, went white middies with black collars and cuffs at the wrist. Full petticoats with a dust ruffle, and camisoles to match, made of nurses' stripe gingham, were required for daily wear. The girls were encouraged to wear dark dresses when not in uniform, which were ordered, custom-made, after the six-week probation period. They were very attractive: black serge with white collars and cuffs.

Kristin did not stay a hayseed for long. Sophomore year she was class secretary, the president during junior and senior years. This occured even though they were, up to that time, the only class to be graduated without officers. How that came about is an interesting story, although the long series of events leading up to it tell something of Kristin and her existence at Sacred Heart.

For, not unlike Phileas in Wyoming Valley, she had come as an "innovation" to the school. Though there were enrolled an ex-Governor's daughter and his niece, as well as other girls of privilege at that time, this farm girl, green as the grass around the one-room school from which she came, brought with her not only an advance inscribed copy of a book by an author the Sisters admired, she was acquainted with the works of many writers, including Oscar Wilde, whom the Catholics had not yet claimed (his *De Profundis* being on the *Index of Forbidden Books*.)

Two months into the year's English class, they had come across a quotation from "The Hound of Heaven" by Francis Thompson. Sister called for a discussion of the lines:

I fled Him down the night and down the days;
        I fled Him down the arches of the years;
I fled Him down the labyrinthine ways
        Of my own mind; and in the midst of tears
I hid from Him, and under running laughter.
            Up vistaed hopes I sped;
            And shot, precipitated,
        Adown Titanic glooms of chasmed fears,
From those strong Feet that followed, followed after.

Kristin raised her hand. "It means," she said, "that Mr. Thompson was rejected for the priesthood and that he became a loose person, a kind of bum, and that God was trying to reclaim him."

"Very, very good," Sister Barbara said. "And tell us where you read that. Surely you read it?"

Edna's engagement picture, 1921

"Yes, the review was in the *Yellow Book*, and then we discussed it."

"The *Yellow Book*?" Sister's voice was a little shrill. "Stay after class. I want to talk with you."

But what was there to reprimand her for, when her mentor had been Father Brudermanns? Kristin explained he had never let her have whole copies of the *Yellow Book*, but had only shared excerpts such as this one.

There was a chaplain who lived in a house on the grounds —a Father Hengell, who had founded the University Chapel. Because of the "Hound of Heaven" episode, and the Durward book (written by his friend) Father Hengell took an interest in Kristin. She liked that.

There were other minor incidents. But not until she came back from Christmas vacation in 1921 were there any shocking reverberations. Kristin returned wearing a diamond engagement ring. Involved was one of those caprices that often change the appearance of things.

Kristin's future husband Peter had chosen for her a beautiful ruby ring, but Mother said a ruby was not a proper engagement symbol, that it had to be a diamond. So they had gone to Dodgeville and exchanged the first ring for a necessarily smaller gem. (Kristin always preferred the ruby.)

Had she been allowed to keep the first one, there might not have been such a hullabaloo. The appearance of an engaged 15-year-old was disturbing to the Irish nuns, by profession aesthetes, by tradition self-contained. It was Father Hengell who told her that some of the Sisters thought she might be a Magdalene! He, on the other hand, accepted her version of the engagement.

Kristin's reception rankled her. It was not uncommon during long Sunday evening devotions for frail young girls to faint. During one of Father Rummell's interminable homilies, a mean thought took root in Kristin's devious mind. Why not? Father Hengell was sitting by in the small sanctuary "saying" (that is, reading) his Office. Kristin keeled over. She had not counted on Father Hengell helping to carry her out of the chapel. Next day, when he saw her, he said, "Spell me the word for that performance last night."

"F-a-i-n-t-i-n-g," Kristin replied.

"More like a 'f-e-i-n-t' eh?"

Instead of denial, she said, "Now they'll think I'm pregnant." His was a great, booming laugh. She knew she had gained, not lost, esteem in his mind. And now it seemed that the drama teacher, whom she liked, no longer looked through her, but at her.

There was plenty of girl-talk during those years. She learned about incest from her room-mate and dearest friend, who later killed herself. There were lesbians at Edgewood, and kleptomaniacs. And there were also the numerous misdemeanors such as fuses blown from cooking in one's room with "donut-heaters." But the class of 1924 was in its final semester when the last confrontation occured.

It seems that Edgewood had the majority of students from affluent families. It was a small school, and this particular senior class numbered about thirty. Besides the high school, there were grades down to fifth.

The Mother Superior at that time was an aristocratic lady from a "Chicago Gold Coast" family, who wanted a finishing school where young ladies learned all the amenities. Consequently, she had arranged a social schedule to wind down the final semester: attendance at a Philadelphia Symphony concert in the University of Wisconsin Stock Pavilion, a tea at the University Club, a reception by the Madison Women's Club, and other ambitious to-dos. "Of course," Mother Superior said, "the non-paying girls who work in the kitchen and at cleaning will not be able to go."

The remark didn't "take" at first, not until the next afternoon. Kristin called a class meeting and the class voted that *everyone* should go to the various functions. In a strict boarding school, one does not question decisions of those in authority (*that* is also a Catholic tradition). The class was ordered to elect a new slate of officers. They refused; Father Hengell, the chaplain, backed the class decision. The upshot was, the class had a really strange *going-out.*

Mother Superior chose all those little props that students think so important: the class flower became the hyacinth, gemstone the zircon, the class play was Shakespeare's *As You Like It*, and even the class motto was chosen by the Mother Superior. From the *Epistle of Paul to the Phillippians*: "Finally, brethern, whatsoever things are true, whatsoever things are honest, whatsoever things are just, whatsoever things are pure, whatsoever things are lovely, whatsoever things are of good report; if there be any virtue, and there be any praise, *think on these things*."

Of course everybody thought it was a putdown, a sort of punishment.

Today Kristin appreciates its beauty and value. And while she thinks they were right to take the stand they did, Mother Superior need not have "gloried in our infirmities," as St. Paul said. Kristin wore a squeaky pair of patent leather shoes to the fanciest reception as a gesture of her rebellion, simply to annoy Mother Superior. Later, raising her own children, she was sorry for that, for failing to understand the lady's position.

During these years, Kristin searched for creative direction. She had four years of piano lessons before Edgewood, but after her second year, one of the music nuns advised her parents to save their money. "All Kristin wants to do is improvise." So much for creativity in 1922.

In sewing class that first year, she made a combing jacket for the St. Patrick's Day Bazaar, and it was still unsold when she left three years later. (A "combing" jacket? Nearly everyone had long hair.) These were made of white terry cloth, sleeveless, and with ribbon ties in front. Kristin's creation was with thousands of French knots, green tendrils, and red sumac leaves. It was an atrocity!

Another search was in Drama. She adored the Sister who taught "Dramatic Art" and she got to play Rosalind, Portia, Joan of Arc, and other roles. She was good in English and History, was an imbecile in algebra, disinterested in geometry. The poor nun who taught mathematics was sorely tried, and passed her with a "D" for desperation. Kristin liked botany so much that her work-books and specimens were used as examples. She also liked Latin and French; the former made her an excellent speller.

As boarders, the girls were allowed to go home at Christmas and Easter. About once a month, they could leave campus to visit a friend's home during daylight hours. On the almost daily walks they were chaperoned.

Kristin loved it at Edgewood, always sat outside the chapel and reveled in the singing of the Dominican "Office." She will never know for sure whether she truly had a vocation to join the convent, or if, subconsciously, she was trying to escape marriage. Or was she simply enamored with the chanting, the modal music that all her life moved her deeply? There was a peace at Edgewood beyond description, a harmony never again to be realized.

Part II

The Halcyon Over the Waves

The Nuptials

It was humorist George Ade, I think, who advised a friend: "If your bride doesn't want an elaborate wedding, look for trouble. She may not be normal." It wasn't until years afterward that I realized how fitting these words were to my life. I begin with them partly because everything connected with marriage has been a trying reminiscence.

Bans for the marriage of Peter Meudt and Edna Kritz had been published and read at all Sunday Masses in St. John's Church, Spring Green, in September and October of 1924. On Tuesday, October 14, following the last announcement, we were married at 8:00 A.M. with no relatives present except their two attendants, Leona Meudt, a cousin, and my brother Leo.

The bride wore black: a wool serge dress, cloche, shoes and hose. I carried no flowers and wore only the engagement ring Peter gave me when I was fifteen. My fashionable mother was disturbed by such choice of attire. It may have been that she understood, better than her daughter, that it was a protest.

That I have preserved my life for eighty-one years, like the petals in the rose jar, should about qualify me to practice the inexact science of psychological analysis. Probably the get-up was a carry-over from Edgewood—those "becoming" black uniforms. For the role of Joan of Arc, I had, eight months before, gladly sacrificed my luxuriant brown-auburn hair. The page-boy style was kept until 1932 and was never again cut. For a few months that previous spring, I *was* Joan of Arc.

How much I lived this I did not understand then, nor in the early ensuing years when I joined FOR (the Fellowship of Reconciliation) and a couple of years later the NAACP. This was ironic. In that depression time I sewed for the family late into the nights, scrimping and saving in other ways, to send support to these organizations. I thought I was still playing Joan of Arc, having not yet recognized my Bohemian grandfather for the pacifist he was.

The marriage ceremony over, we went to a cafe for coffee and doughnuts, then returned to the house in Wyoming Valley where a wedding feast had been prepared. The table was set for eight, the two extras being Peter's father, Frank, and his brother, William. Mother had outdone herself to make it festive. She put out monogrammed linens, the best china and silver, the last five roses of summer for centerpiece. A bouquet of aster and dahlias was in the parlor. There were roasted capons with dressing, cloud-light angel food cake, and a fruit parfait that could have upstaged Julia Child.

At this late date I wonder if the in-laws thought this a prefiguration of meals to come! I had never baked bread or pies, and knew nothing about meats. All I knew was the taste of good food . . . and I could read. Mother had given me a *White House Cook Book*, 1924 vintage. The frontispiece picture is of Grace Goodhue Coolidge, the reigning first lady of the time.

Between 2:30 and 3:00 we took off in Peter's new Buick, a big touring car for which he had traded in his sporty roadster, a Ford with wire wheels. We drove to Arena to pick up Mr. and Mrs. Carl Meudt who were also wed that day, a ten o'clock full regalia nuptials. We were travelling together to Saint Paul where cousins Marie and Margaret lived, and where the other bride, Arlene, also had relatives.

Arlene had taught school for several years, Carl was a World War I veteran. When Peter (who was my mother's partner in trickery to achieve our union) saw them together, so obviously in love—did he think, as I did: "This is how it should be!" Was he so enamored as to be blind to our reality? Five years older than I, that inexperienced?

For reasons known only to whatever fates arrange such tragicomedies, we got only as far as Tomah where the grooms decided, in circumstances dissimilar to those of Brigham Young: *This is the Place.*

It was a prosperous-looking town, which even then had lush green medians and many trees in glorious foliage. The hotel they chose was the best, with a fine dining room. Our room on the second floor had a veranda from which could be seen the steeple of St. Mary's Church where Father Brudermanns was pastor. (He who left Spring Green, rather than officiate at this marriage, which he thought to be wrong, likely sensing that it would be ill-fated.)

At the door to our room, hand on the knob, I told Peter I needed time alone, that I was going for a walk. Here at least one of the Fates smiled on me. Peter seemed to understand. That I needed a lot of letting alone became a pattern in our lives. He respected that as few men might have. Maybe he knew there was no other choice: he deserves the benefit of doubt.

Above the street lights the harvest moon hung, imposing, like an oriental gong. It lent an eeriness to the places I walked, careful to keep the spire in view, so as not to get lost. In an hour or so I tired and came back to a small park near the hotel. I found a bench and began a mental inventory of what had taken me to this stage.

I was a normally curious young girl in good health. I half-believed the Valley wives-tales that natural affection came with the intimacies of marriage and that love would come with children. I was less innocent than ignorant. Or, subconsciously I may have wanted to leave the Valley, with its early sundowns and the interminable nights which an insomniac endures.

(It was true, I'd wanted to return to Madison, find work and later go to an art school. Circumstance had rendered that an impossibility—along with, I was to find later on, collusions.) Such being the case, the gorgeous vistas of Pleasant Ridge offered alternatives. We would live on a farm among all the well-to-do Meudts, the first of whom had settled there prior to the Civil War.

Inventory, but no answers. I had childlike faith in a personal God who cared and would make things right: strong feelings that all the commandments were valid, even those concerning mother and father and neighbor; that up there in that moon there was real magic. I remembered when I was nine, then also in a strange town—wide awake next to my mother in Aunt Annie's house in Dodgeville. Everyone was snoring, Mother loudest of all. Downstairs, Uncle Lew was sitting with Baba. "It is nearing her time to go," they had said. Out the window was this same great February moon, almost scarlet. I lay there hoping the moon might be a kind of way station where Baba could rest on her way to Heaven. (Or could it be Purgatory itself?)

When I woke to breakfast smells, Uncle Lew had left, as farmers do, with daily chores. That was why we were there—Mother taking Father's place, helping out. I was mouthing oatmeal when someone knocked at the kitchen door. Mother looked at the clock. "It's that wonderful boy, Peter, on his way to school, I'll bet."

He came in, cap in hand, every hair in place. He gave a box to Aunt Annie. "How is Mrs. Kritz this morning? Mother and Grandma said I should tell you they're praying for her." There was more, plus exclamations over the rich molasses-ginger cookies he had brought, but politely refused to sample, saying, "Those are for you."

After his leave-taking, there was small talk over coffee, time for good gossip. Aunt Annie said: "It's the only way we know what's going on in this world." There were words of praise for Peter's mother, Ellen, for her fine sewing: "Small wonder her sons are always so well-dressed!" She was also a perfect housekeeper.

I tired of this and went to look in on Baba, who was sleeping after a wakeful night. Her room was dark and smelled strange. I did not stay for long.

The next afternoon Father came to sit with his mother; we would be going home that evening. Mother took me uptown for a little shopping and then we paid a visit to Father Ambauen. On the way home, under that same watchful moon, I fell asleep in the cozy sleigh box. Baba died that same week.

In that little park, the fateful passing-over of years seemed like a low-budget movie. Now I was fourteen, home from Edgewood for Easter vacation. We would spend the Holiday with Aunt Annie, now living with her daughter, Mary, who was married to Fred Meudt. Sitting on that bench in Tomah, should I have forgotten that "wonderful boy, Peter," now eighteen, was working for his Uncle Fred? Or that all the next summer, my mother developed an unusual interest in attending Mass at the mission church on Pleasant Ridge?

Before I returned to Edgewood, we had four "dates." On one of these, Peter said to me, "If my mother had not died when I was sixteen, I would have gone to college and probably would never have looked at you." (He was the first of several to reap from me, for remarks like *that*, a bitter harvest of words.)

Now the town clock tolled eleven. The sky was like a mirror backed with black. The girl who I was went in to her bridegroom as for centuries on centuries, billions of girls have done. The pattern is infinite—forever and ever without end? Except, in this case, on that very night, a son was conceived. And a child, any child, is unlike any other, is an incantation as much as incarnation, in a special flesh. The person that child becomes is unique and will remain so as long as there are those who remember.

Pleasant Ridge

Those seven years were composed of amaranth and day lilies. They were, as Wilde once wrote, one very long moment. Suffering, I had come to believe, was the means by which one became conscious of existing. Not that working mothers have it easier today; theirs is a different lifestyle in another era. I see the same signs of stress in them, sense their frustrations, not unlike mine (the saddest of which was that there was so little time for the mothering of my young children. This was before "baby sitting" became a commonplace).

The dowry I brought on November 1st to the big square house on Pleasant Ridge consisted of a fancy new bedroom suite, a large cedar chest filled with linens and things. Ànd two cats—Sarah and Bozo. Why do I remember that all the lamp chimneys were smoky? Because they added to the late afternoon overcast. Otherwise the house was clean.

Though the men (Peter, his father Frank and brother Willie) had moved to the farm on March 1st, the large central room was still piled ceiling-high with furniture. In the downstairs room the new suite was in place, and upstairs there was a bed and chair in each room. The kitchen was barely functional, with a wood stove, a dry sink, table and four chairs. There was a small pantry with shelves. First thing I bought was a large kitchen cabinet, a marvel of compressed efficiency. It has a metal flour bin (50 pounds), a metal sugar bin (25 pounds), a roll-type compartment for spices; under the enameled-iron counter is a pull-out cutting board. There were shelves for dishes, and compartment below the counter for pots and pans. It was purchased, mail-order, from Sears with wedding gift money. I am still using it every day.

There must have been, fifteen years before my arrival, a fire sale somewhere in the vicinity. I am allowing myself a vulgarity here. The whole interior of that house, wainscoting (probably hard maple or walnut), sidewalls, ceilings, were what can only be described as shit-brindle, streaked as they were with wear and smoke. Before Christmas brother-in-law Willie and I gave the whole downstairs two coats of pale beige. Frank and Ellen had nice furniture; with it in place, we had a home. With Christmas gift money from Father Brudermanns, I bought an Aladdin mantle lamp, my solution to night-gloom.

But we were twelve years away from the Rural Electrification Act of 1936. It seems such a simple declaration to say that today! Of what it signified in drudgery the less said the better. (A quip comes to mind. "We used to be told that Adam and Eve invented sin. Now we know it was Edison." He should be the patron saint of rural housewives!)

That first was a winter of learning more than of discontent. Moving the buffet in place, I opened a drawer to find letters, written by my mother, that Peter was to have destroyed. Reading them, I understood how and why our broken engagement had been mended. Before coming home from Edgewood I had written him that I wanted out, insured the ring I'd had for three years and mailed it back to him. Mother was cool to me during the rest of June, all of July and the first week of August. But during that time, when we were in Spring Green or Dodgeville, Peter kept showing up. I let him drive me home in his new Buick, but did not relent; the plans were all revealed in those letters.

All plans but one. That last meeting I felt sorry for him; he was suffering and I was to blame. He went home and tried to hang himself. Were it not for that smart dog, Major, alerting Willie, he might have succeeded. I have here reported it for the first time, an incident so painful that it was blotted out on the bench in the Tomah park but not during those difficult early years of marriage. To this day I feel that the Lord was "twisting my tripes," to use the words of Justice Holmes.

Those days I learned that an efficient farm woman has her wash on the lines early and "white as the driven snow," that her floors should be "clean enough to eat off of" (I never figured out why) and that the stoves were to be as "black as Toby" (he was the only Black person near).

My father never swore, Leo occasionally. The Meudt men were prodigious oath-makers. Their swearing tempered me for acceptance of widespread profanities of later generations.

Neighborliness took on new dimensions. The aunts and cousins were kind, far beyond their duty. There were times I could not have managed without their help, and during those early years I never had to ask.

Meat had to be processed for warm weather use; four or five hogs were butchered at one time. Hams and half the shoulders for the smokehouse; the rest was to be "fried down" and stored in three-gallon crocks. Heads, livers, hearts, were made into sausage, and lastly the fat was rendered into lard. There was the heavy work of canning in two-quart mason jars of three quarters of a beef. One quarter or more was eaten fresh. Then there were the threshing, shredding and silo-filling crews to be fed.

Ours was the only one-woman household on the Ridge. The Meudt women came, taking turns. My eyes brim as I write, for I can never thank them enough. Wherever you are, Aunts Lena, Mary, Anna, Katie Meudt and Aunt Julia Davis: *thank you*!

The fourth Spring Willie and Hazel Buttens, a neighbor girl, were married. We divided the house space. Things were looking up! I was expecting a third child. Mercifully, Frank took his meals with them.

Frank did not like me; the feeling was mutual. With good reason, my first ineptitudes galled him. Two of them stand out.

The farm owners from whom we rented came one weekend from Rockford, unannounced. They were husband, wife, and three of their five children. The larder was skimpy. The eldest son and I with the help of Major, the dog, ran down two young roosters. (Major enjoyed those fresh heads.) I took the chickens out back of the house to scald and remove feathers, and to singe them with a quick blaze of newspaper.

In the night someone wakened to a strange glow in the sky; the woodpile out in back was on fire. There must have been a hollow piece at the base, where the chickens were singed, that acted as a flue. Frank had always made a large circular wall with the round chunks for the heating stove, which he filled with split wood for the cooking range. This time, only half the wood was saved.

Another time, hastily changing his bed, I left the coverings too close to the stovepipe that went from floor to ceiling in his room, and a quilt which Ellen had made was scorched. It took awhile to live down such episodes.

Frank suffered from asthma and almost every evening, inhaled smoke from a powder called Asthmador; this may have contributed to his unpleasant disposition. For years I carried a guilt that mine was simply a case of "I do not like thee, Doctor Fell. . . ." However, fairly recently, Hazel said, "I still get a tight feeling when I think about Bill's dad." (After Willie and Hazel's marriage, he was no longer called "Willie" but "Bill.") "The closer I came to the house after I'd been away, the heavier the lump in my chest, just thinking about him."

I exonerate myself somewhat when incidents are recalled. I will relate but one: Speaking his displeasure with me to his sister Mary, he said, "I put a kitchen match in the wash basin every night to check if she washes herself in the morning." This revelation did nothing for our relationship. And I was careful he not discover my personal basin hidden in the pantry.

Nonetheless, Frank was shrewd and thrifty, and because of his astute investments, I have been able to spend a half century in this wonderful location—a farm on which he held the mortgage.

Happenings in my life have to do with gardens. I really do feel "closer to God in a garden." And I do not relish the thought of not having one to putter in, though mine today is but a patch compared to previous ones. I do not have to search for reasons to go outside.

One Spring day when I was thirteen, weeding the seed onions and carrots, the mailman brought the letter saying I'd been accepted at Edgewood. I also think that the garden has a relationship to my childbearing. On my second and third births, working among the vegetables, labor was thus facilitated. For the first baby it was clearly happenstance.

June 25, 1925: we had been a couple of weeks without rain. The garden was screaming for attention which I had foolishly hoped might be forthcoming from one of the men. Breakfast over, there was a far distant rumbling in the west. I left the dishes and hurried to the garden and worked like a maniac. The electrical storm moved to the north, but some rain fell. It was warm and I was glad for the shower.

When the sun came out it was almost directly above. Noon! And men to be fed. I dug some early cobbler potatoes, snatched some parsley for cream gravy and started for the house. The back porch steps had needed to be rebuilt since the first time I stepped on them. Now, exhausted, awkward, heavy, when I was

Edna, 1926

on the top step, it caved in. It is a wonder the baby was not maimed or killed, for a large bruise soon showed on me where his head must have lain. I was not able to prepare the meal but did get supper on the table.

Nauseous and woozy, I had what was the first of innumerable migraines. About ten o'clock cramps began, though I was not "due" for two weeks and four days. Taking some aspirin, I fell asleep, not to waken until around two in the morning, with a sudden realization that "it" was happening; labor had begun.

What did I think about, initially? That now my mother, always sin-suspicious, would be sure that she was right. It was my lot, then, and each time after, to "show" after the third month of pregnancy. This so worried me that I did not waken Peter until daylight. Had I been rational and not under stress, I would have remembered those three weeks when the bans of matrimony were announced. I was still that obedient and somewhat frightened school girl.

Richard Edward Meudt was born at home at 2:00 P.M. Then began the six-weeks siege: Tracy Meudt and Aunt Julia Davis took weekly turns while the baby cried most of the time. My milk had almost no nourishment. It took Tracy, the eldest of all the cousins and an "old maid," to solve the problem. "This baby is starving," she said, showing the menfolk Richard's thumb and forefinger, from which the skin had been sucked. "One of you has to go to town and get nursing bottles and Mellon's Food Formula. Now! Not tomorrow!"

Richard had eight ounces at five, another feeding at ten, and everyone had a full night's sleep. At breakfast, I overhead Tracy telling the men: "When he woke up at seven he was smiling. And if I thought you'd believe it, I'd swear he winked at me."

Bedridden for those torrid July days, there was again time for me to read. Through the notebooks from Edgewood, I rediscovered Pere Lacordaire, in which I found a passage which dealt with the importance of "A clean heart before God and Self. Never mind about your Neighbor." Lacordaire did not admire human respect. I quit caring that my baby came a little early.

Womanhood was beginning to flower. I refused to be "Churched," a ceremony in which the "delivered" is met at the church door by the priest to be blessed and purified. I said to Father Ambauen, "Why me and not Peter? I was uncomfortable for months, the premature birth of a ten-pound child was difficult, and I've been unable to walk for six weeks. Isn't suffering purification?" He acquiesced, probably thinking of me as the four-year old he had baptized, and having been so long a heathen.

My old fascination with animals and nature returned in odd ways. Soon after my arrival, the dog, Major, wanting no traffic with cats, killed Sarah. She was small and delicate, but Bozo was not; he was part Abyssinian with streaks of gray, and was not about to be done in. After a couple of good fights, I took him inside to be a household pet. With a cross baby and a sick woman and all the other work, the visiting ladies consistently chased Bozo with the broom. By the time I was up and about, he had disappeared. I missed him greatly and thought him but another casualty of lost youth. Then one very cold evening in mid-November, when I was alone in the house, there was a scratching at the door. It was Bozo, home after a summer and fall in the woods below the house, fat and looking like a woodchuck. It was a happy reunion!

The mores of that time were different where babies were concerned, though swaddling had been discontinued. Richard was five months old and my mother wanted to show him off at the pre-Thanksgiving potluck of the Wyoming Valley Ladies Aid. When we got to her house, she was waiting, so we left immediately.

I always thought him the best looking of my children. (Everyone did not agree.) Aunt Julia had knitted him a blue woolen outfit: sweater, cap and a knee-length romper with booties to match. Someone else had given us a white lamb's wool shawl. I became aware that every time his fat, pink knees were exposed, my mother would reach over to cover them with the shawl. Finally I said, "You don't have to do that. It's really warm in here."

She said: "He isn't wearing stockings. Where are the white lisle stockings I gave him?" Obviously this was a faux pas.

I will also tell of a bridge I built over a seemingly dry gully: When Richard was six months old, he grew afraid of lady's hats. I could no longer sit with him on the side for females in the Mission Church. He was also terrified by the farm animals. He carried his Tot Walker around with him at least four months, when he could have walked on his own. I worried, thinking my fall on the porch steps had something to do with producing an original Caspar Milquetoast. But the day he turned eighteen, he enlisted in a deadly war, stayed twenty years in the Navy, where he went from gunner on an aircraft carrier to deepsea diver at Pearl Harbor. He was a chief deputy in law enforcement when he died.

These were the years in incubation for bureaucracy. Surely it was an ill-conceived ploy to cut down on milk production and its by-products: the tuberculin decimation of dairy cattle took our entire herd of forty-nine head. Even nationally, financial recovery from the depression was a good ways off. In our instance, it was a long, long ways off. Throughout our area, the first years of the thirties were notable for the worst drought in history.

Bad luck seems to like to travel in company. Peter, against his father's advice (and mine) traded the Buick for an elegant Pontiac. When the herd went, the car was repossessed. My father bought us a good used Chevrolet on the condition I learn to drive. Unfortunately, it was an expectation I did not fulfill.

Frank's patience and savings had been depleted by the purchasing of hay and grain during the drought. There is great irony in buying expensive feed for livestock soon to be destroyed. A sardonic afterthought: tumors showed up in only about one-third of the cows! True, the farmers were reimbursed less than half-value, or so they claimed, but the checks were quite a while coming. We all began to know what Hard Times were in the country!

Edna and children Howard, Kathleen, and Richard

Where is the Halcyon in all this? Sometimes flying high, sometimes low. How and when could it be otherwise? But ever present were the simple joys, those commonplaces so frequently overlooked. Small boys provided many of these, and I ask that you keep in mind George Ade's words with which this chapter begins. I was "non-normal" enough to relish daring and innovativeness in my little ones.

This particular corn-shredding time, Kathleen was an infant. Richard and Howard were four and three. When the men left the house after the noon meal, they saw the two of them walking around on the windmill platform, a space fourteen inches wide and at least twenty-five feet in the air. There was quick consultation. The children were often afraid of Peter, so it was decided that Uncle Jake, our closest neighbor and their special favorite, should climb the metal ladder and bring them down. I can still feel their excitement as they were telling me about being up so high. I would not permit scolding or punishment, but had the men remove the bottom section of the attached ladder.

They were as inseparable as twins and had, at that time, a language of their own not easily understood, except by them. Less than a year apart in age, they started school together. Howard was the taller. (When he died at ten years, six months, he required a man-sized casket.) He had a pretty voice and at their first Thanksgiving program, he sang a solo, during which he forgot a few lines, and had to be prompted. Afterwards, the teacher took me aside to admonish: "If the boys weren't an hour or more late every day, this might not have happened. We practiced for the program in the morning."

Mystified and amused, we confronted the wayward ones. The school bell rang at 8:30 and, three-quarters of a mile away, I'd always sent them off in plenty of time. They admitted to spending the time fishing and looking for rabbits along a gentle creek that burbled under the small bridge they had to cross.

Kathleen, then my youngest, changed Frank's life, mellowed him. Not only was she a beautiful child, but she reminded him of his late wife. He was ever at her bidding; a really deep attachment was between them. He died in August, one month after she was four. When her brothers went to school, she often cried for Grandpa. He was a very short man, and she could never transfer that affection to my six-foot-four father. Five months later, we went to live for two months with my parents, and she found a grandmother to love.

At the end of that December, the farm's owners, due to job loss in Rockford, came back to their home place, and since farm occupancy for renters was never available until March 1st, my folks took us in. It was a bountiful vacation for me; taking advantage of child care, I had some uncritical but overdue surgery at Madison General Hospital. (This was the last time I visited the Coyne home on Milton Street, where I'd spent many Sundays while at Edgewood. Anna Coyne was at University of Wisconsin Medical School. Her brother, Father Dan, helping out at St. Raphaels, was there for awhile on Saturday evening and again on Sunday before returning to Dubuque. Afterward, we began corresponding regularly.)

The Three Years Interim

We had supposed we'd be on the interim place for no more than a year. We were that naive about the turning of legal wheels and government regulations. Bill and Hazel were to inherit a farm near Edmund. It took three years for them, and for us, to obtain possession, to finally settle in.

Practicality had dictated that these temporary locations be small. Actually ours was an adjunct to a large operation. There was a house on this second farm which was near Ridgeway and it had been vacant for awhile. It was a little more than a shelter in which we figured we could camp for a winter. Farm owners are not keen on short-term tenants.

Doctor William Reese was our landlord. He was a careful business man, so how had this been managed? One can never be sure of another's motives. He was a bachelor and perhaps took a deeper interest in his "children?" And a more profound one in such as me, for it was his wise perception in prescribing a placebo rather than ergot that steered my safe passage into the world.

What happened during those years was that I began to manifest myself. Doctor Reese, as I wrote in the poem "Fulcrum," made it possible for me to gain a kind of knowledge that gave strength, a circular view of life. Without his knowing, he pointed me toward an insight into the Holy Spirit.

In that place, the other person who came into my life gave me, truly, a second birth. I began to know, as T.S. Eliot wrote, that "the past has another pattern and ceases to be mere sequence."

This second *life* began to come into being on a March day, raw with bluster: Father Dan Coyne was at the door. "Surprise!" he greeted me, adding that he was enroute to Madison for a synod on curriculum for seminarians.

During first shock I was glad that this time the poor kitchen was clean, that it was fragrant with freshly-baked bread and cinnamon rolls melting their sugar to gloss. The children were in school; Peter had taken a grist to the mill. With trembling hands I served refreshment, managed to pour the coffee, reacting to his magnetism as always before. With food on the table, lifetimes waited; our exchanged amenities fell fast-frozen. For me, the room and all its artifacts disappeared.

So even though we still had no home we could call our own, these were an eventful three years for me, spiritually. We did buy a Bosch radio, and via the airwaves I traveled, feasted on music and literature, had time to read. And I was in love for the first time.

This Home on the Hill

We came in 1936 to this uplands farm that Henry Dodge had chosen as the place he wanted to live. I can no longer recall when I first felt this honored pioneer man's presence. Perhaps, these days, it is most often when his woods south of our house takes on the green blush of Spring.

Somewhat as Dodge had, we came here as a haven from inimical circumstance: before moving, at the urging of Peter, to the farm on Pleasant Ridge, Frank had been a teamster in Dodgeville, engaged in the lucrative work of excavation and drayage. The men to whom Frank had loaned money managed to weasel out of much that was due the estate. Litigations took more, and both farms were assessed at considerably higher value. "Prosperity was just around the corner!"—but not for us.

The first fifteen months brought the death of a son, Howard, and the birth of our daughter Christine (about whom the short story "Yesterdays" was written, with some poetic license. She was *not* a child of the depression.)

I have never rid myself of a sense of fatalistic exchange in connection with these two events: an insomniac at all other times, but during pregnancies, I slept like one drugged. Add to that, this child shared her uterine chamber with numerous fibroid tumors. I was sure she would be deformed, retarded, or both. Ah, the useless worries! She was quite perfect.

But had I not been so toxic I would have wakened and divined how ill Howard was that night, realized the medicine a doctor had prescribed for stomach flu was not right, and his appendix would not have ruptured. "The saddest words of tongue or pen: it might have been."

Years sped along like highway traffic and the planes above. The day the Bomb was dropped on Hiroshima, I was "coming to" after grave surgery. The Call was closer than any of those in the Valley had been. Were I not in the hands of Doctor Harris, who had delivered Christine, there would be one less poet in Wisconsin.

The John W. Harris Obstretrical and Gynecological Society honoring his memory was later organized in that department of the University of Wisconsin which he had established in 1928. How many women and their families also praise his memory, I can only estimate, but this I know: few need be as grateful as I.

Hearing the discussion among the operating room personnel, I truly wanted to retreat into the tunnel from which they were trying to save me. And I had the strangest sense that if I crossed over, I'd see Richard (no, not Howard) who was serving in that area of the Pacific. But that is a tale for telling another time.

What of all these other years for my children, always for them the time of growing up? Were they ever-loving and obedient? Each were in their turn, of course, engaged in escapades with peers. I think they had fair portions of happiness and the usual hurts and disappointment. They each became responsible adults and they knew sorrows and tragedy firsthand. I hope that they did not interpret as uncaring or indifference an attitude of mine —they never received "free advice." I had suffered too much so-called "guidance."

My own girlhood had been so rigidly manipulated that I may have leaned too far the other direction. When asked for advice, I seemed too often to surmise they were not going to heed what I had to offer and so replied: "Make your own mistakes. It may be less fun having no one to blame but yourself, but you won't forget so easily."

Some of the recent winter was spent in sorting old papers, looking into dusty storeroom boxes. In one was Mother's annotated King James Bible. It is in poor condition, some pages almost worn away. In it were two of my letters. One of these, I thought, really encapsulates my life during these years.

June 15, 1943

Dear Mother and Dad,

Your card came this morning and I'm sorry, Dad, that you are feeling so poorly. I know that the way Peter is makes you unhappy but I can do nothing. If I could, he would be speaking to Richard, who says he's going to enlist as soon as he's eighteen. That's only ten days off! Say some prayers (you too, Mother) that he'll change his mind. I don't want him in this God-awful war!

I didn't intend writing till Thursday but this noon we heard the warning over WIBA about the Wisconsin River. Of course we're hoping to be able to cross and you can look for us on Sunday. If the river is well over the road don't expect us. Richard isn't that sure of the road bed. If Father Dan comes, we'll make special effort.

I was going to make a birthday cake for Dad but when you said you're having homemade strawberry shortcake I changed my plans. I'll try to find a good watermelon to bring, instead.

So you heard my name over WGN for me to receive 8 ozs. cheese? I'm insulted. I wouldn't compete for such a small prize. I'm supposed to get two pounds of fancy cheeses and a wooden lazy-susan with a big glass center dish with six separations. I don't really deserve anything. I've a book, "Recipes from all over the World." The "Danish Tymbals" recipe came from it. I'll probably sizzle for such deception. I'll bring the book.

The corn is up high enough so that they are cultivating today. The crops look very good. Did you have a terrible storm on Sunday night? We had the worst one in a long while. Christine and I were in the cellar but Kathleen and Richard would have no part of that. (I must clean that basement.) I wish this fear of storms would go away.

The carpenters have been here a few days again, putting in the feeding floor, partitions and stanchions. And a sidewalk to the kitchen; they are finished for awhile and I take back what I said about them running us out of staples. They brought their number 13 Sugar Stamps, each entitling us to five pounds, and they gave me several blue Tokens. (Bacon.) Also they deducted $3.00 per day for their two meals. I can't make money much easier.

The girls and I went to Madison a week ago with Father Dan to see his brother, Tom, in the hospital. I don't think he'll get better but he knew us and was so brightened to see Christine. Too bad he and Lydia never had children. He loves little ones so much. Lydia was a nervous wreck: Some special person had come in and they needed Tom's private room so they up and moved him in with a pneumonia patient. She wasn't getting much action but when Father Dan used some diplomacy, Tom was moved back.

Kathleen got a pretty string knit bathing suit and Christine a castle for her goldfish and some other trinkets. Madison is no place for bargains, but I hunted up some pliers for Peter. Shortages, shortages! Had my scissors sharpened also. Have you heard that soap will be rationed when the new booklets are out? They need the naptha for explosives. There is no laundry soap in the cities but in the towns there's some, still to be nabbed.

The yard is lovely, peonies in full bloom, and the garden is producing.

Hoping to see you on Sunday, and love to both of you.

Edna

Yesterdays

Anne is polishing the silver for a party—her *party*. Tomorrow she will be sixteen. Her footsteps are the echoes of my heartbeats.

"Grandmother, what did you use for this in the old days?"

"Death is the original tarnish-remover," I reply absent-mindly. I run the steam iron over the last strip of the fourth skirt of nylon tulle and taffeta and slip the formal off the board.

"You left that awful flower on, and you know I'm going to have to have an orchid for the dance tomorrow night . . . Did you say 'Death,' Grandmother? Who wants to talk about that!"

"I was thinking aloud, my dear . . . We used powdered hartshorn on a chamois skin." I am humming an old tune.

"Why, Grandma, that's number five on Record Round-Up this month. Are you the sharpie! Hartshorn and Hit-tunes!" When she smiles, Anne is beautiful.

"I learned it when I was your age. It is Opus number something or other. It was composed by Robert Schumann."

"You played it on the jew's harp, or the mouth organ?"

"Neither. We had an organ—a violin. Uncle Paul has it still—the violin I mean."

She shakes her head. "I guess I can't imagine you having

The Meudt residence near Dodgeville

nice things. Everything was so *primitive* when you were young—primitive here in the midwest. We've been reading about weaving, and butter-making, and kerosene lamps, and *sadirons*!" Anne looks superior despite her pin-curls and gaudy T-shirt. I cannot suppress myself.

"Shouldn't we both laugh?" she asks with a little edge to her voice.

"All right. Turn your temper switch to 'simmer,' and I'll tell you. Your mother said such things to me, too. Perhaps not as emphatically, but those days were difficult, and some people would say her dissatisfaction—or shall we call it distrust of the past—was more understandable."

"Don't tell me *you* don't think we're impossible and spoiled like everyone else does!"

"No. And I didn't think your mother was either. I stood up to my waist in life with Diana there on the edge—in the shallows—with the eternal problem of parenthood confronting me."

"What problem?" she asks.

"Of remembering, of reaching her—remembering not to

confuse place with personality. Understanding that I must go back to reach her, and that if she tried to cross me, I would lose her."

"What did you do?"

"I wrote her a letter for her sixteenth anniversary; we talked about it the day we planned this party for you." I sit staring.

"Grandmother, go on—what about the letter?"

"She still has it. If I tell you we intend to give it to you tomorrow, I have spoiled the *surprise*."

"Surprise! An old letter a surprise? Then don't tell me! Let me be overwhelmed."

Very gently, I ask, "What would *you* consider a surprise, Anne dear?" She is thinking fast; then she blushes. I continue, "A motor boat, 70 miles from the nearest river—a plane to give the farm an air of sophistication—you have cars and radios and television and beautiful clothes and everything your comfort requires."

"Sorry. I was just being smarty—or not thinking, I guess. I'd like to have mother's letter from you."

"But there are more. You will have one from your Uncle Paul too."

"No, no!" she cries, "I'm getting a polaroid camera from him . . . I hinted."

I ignore her. "And one from me—a letter, not a camera."

"Golly, Grandma; it's my birthday. Will I get another thing done but read letters?" Of Diana's children, only Anne has the pointed tongue, the impatient approach—it is the basis of our kinship.

"Your birthday was sixteen years ago. Tomorrow is the anniversary of that momentous event," I say.

"All right, then, I am a bantam brain. Don't bother with me."

"I am only in up to my neck now. I can see you where your mother stood twenty-one years ago. I had still rather struggle back and see how it feels than complain that you are shallow."

"Oh Grandma!" There is a catch in her voice.

"Run along, darling. I must write your letter now, because I waited for Paul's. It came this afternoon and I had to open it to see how he began our voyage into yesterday. Otherwise, I wouldn't know where to join you. You don't mind, Anne?"

"Of course not. It was your very own idea." She leaves me.

It is a long way back. It is like clearing out an attic, such strange shards in the debris, tomes that have been carelessly or ruthlessly buried. So we come into conflict with the past from which we must be severed. One thing lives, another dies. Like Siamese twins, the past and future lie sick on the same bed. It has come to this.

Pheasant West, Wisconsin
May 28, 1931

Dear Diana:

This morning on my way home from town, I stopped at the place where I was born. The farm has been without a tenant for three years. The talk is that Mr. Albright will lose it. Our old log house withstands the ravages of neglect quite well, but the roof on the barn is almost gone and the sheep-shed has fallen in. This will seem to you a strange place for anyone to go—even more strange to have gone there for comfort.

These are "hard times," as your grandparents would have said; we call it a depression. It does not matter. Only the scenes change. The struggle and the heartaches are the same. We wanted you to have so much and there is almost nothing to do with. The country is burned dry and the crops cannot possible be much good now. We do not expect the chickens to do well or the cows to give milk when earth offers them almost nothing to eat. My dear, you must be patient with us, too.

Today I went to the spring back of the house. For a short while I was a child again. The oak tree gave of its cool and soundless shade. The water was sweet and sparkling as in that far yesterday when I played beside it.

I pulled a big box full of watercress for the hens. The under shoots will be used for salad. The stone on which I knelt to gather the cress had 1860 hewn into it by someone unknown.

Afterward, when I sat back to rest, my knees were embossed 0981, with the 9 turned upside-down and backward.

It was then that I was aware that my father was near. I had not been praying, though one must, in a sense, know a pilgrimage as prayer.

I wept then from worry and disappointment, and I am telling you so that you may be spared these futile acts which I performed for you. We wanted you to have pretty things and laughter and your young friends around you, and all you will have tomorrow is a cotton dress and a cake with colored icing—both of which were made for you this afternoon. And a letter, this letter, written as a legacy on the eve of your sixteenth birthday anniversary.

Father's family came from the land of music—Bohemia, his birthplace. While he was an infant, the family moved to rural southwestern Wisconsin. But there were too many thorns and thistles to be good for barefooted children.

This immigrant family, that eventually numbered twelve, scraped enough together to buy several cows. How that hilly sub-marginal farm sustained so many children and so few cows is hard to imagine. On frosty mornings, bringing cows in from the woods for milking, they were glad for the issue from the animals in which to warm their feet. That belongs in your family history. It is not told to be uncouth. If it is abhorrent, blame the clumsiness of my language.

I could have described instead a Christmas in Father's childhood, had not Hamlin Garland done that too well for it ever to need redoing by me. Some day you will read his "First Christmas Tree."

Father was one of the most naturally refined persons I have ever known. This gentleness even told on his livestock. Those that were not tame showed no dislike for human companionship. None of them were as clever or social-conscious as those in the cartoons, but they were real.

There was his old dog, Sport. Your grandfather was seldom without apples in his pockets, never without a jackknife.

Whimsy or courtesy made him offer to share with the animals he happened to be with—in the case of a team of horses, an apple divided. Sport always ate the cores. Across the years I can still feel the companionship that existed between the tall man and his two children and the collie dog. Today I almost put out my hand to that once-loved servant. It seemed he must come and nuzzle me, his bronze coat giving off a fadeless light.

It is hard to explain a man like Father—the things he went without in order to buy books which are today treasured possessions. He used the old walking plow years longer than necessary so that we could purchase a "talking machine" and discs, and after some winding and waiting, they filled our parlor with such arias as "I Dreamt I Dwelt in Marble Halls." With radio and movies the marble halls have become fairly common. It is the dreams that are getting scarce.

You are beginning to study about conservation. There is a National Resources Planning Board, and people talk of it as something revolutionary. Your grandfather was a conservationist, though he was one of those who stripped the land of its timber—perhaps unwisely at times. This knowledge comes the same way I sense that my grandparents' hearts must have ached in their exile for the sweetness of Bedrich Smetana's music. How else could their son have enshrined it in mine? Had his heart not bled even as he felled the trees and grubbed the stumps and burned over the best berry patch, his child could not feel these things so deeply.

Today just outside of town a CCC crew were watering the little dried-up evergreens. What an ugly sight these class-conscious, planned forests, where never a cottonwood caresses the brow of a pine—what an ugly sight they will be in the new era of equality and brotherhood. But no uglier than the thought of a young Joe Juniper, shovel in hand, planting trees that have been handed to him in a damp burlap bag, vague on all but one aspect of the whole project: the smug notion that he is performing an act of atonement, having heard how lustily grandpa raped the virgin timber.

Before any embryo forester is allowed to plant a tree, he should know that Plato was writing about conservation around

500 B.C., and he should have a long course on why his forebears behaved as they did, and what that behavior purchased in terms of present day enlightenment. Railroad ties hauled ten miles to town several times a week all winter purchased musical instruments, books, etc., that would have served ten children as well as two.

I have not written of Mother, because she is with us and your remembrance of her must be your own. Fathers, mothers, lovers must be dead to be completely appreciated. Some will tell you that this is the irony of life, while others accept it as the full expression of life. I do not know. I do know that memories of Father have a special flavor.

Hand in hand, we looked far away down the haunting valleys that promised so much. On my sixteenth anniversary I saw for the first time how incongruous with his patrician face were his workworn hands—because they were lifeless. My admiration for him is the closest thing to love you will ever feel for him. Wear it proudly. For the *rest* of us, wear your gown and mantle of goodness and happiness always—tomorrow and forever. We love you.

Your Mother

Milwaukee, Wisconsin
September 19, 1955

Dear Anne:

If this letter is late, your grandmother will not be pleased. I have been in the hospital for eight days. When she hears what I did, she may scold me. It is hard for a fellow like me to be cautious. Some day, not so far away, perhaps, she can say, "Paul Brozek! Surely I knew him! He was my brother. They found him in the arms of death, caught while he was still struggling to write a lost verse. Well, he was always caught in some sweet difficulty, so why not by sweet death herself?"

But what will you say of me? Will you remember Mother Gopher whom we watched last summer? Such a pretty little threshold, a small flat stone swept clean by a gopher's tail! There the mistress sat by the door with arms folded, dreaming in the sun. We watched her go to the store to get a few seeds and leaves. She didn't fuss and fix up like most women, but wore her checkered kitchen apron to the store like any sensible farm woman. She made me lonesome.

All I *meant* to tell you is that I went to the State Fair. It was the first I have attended in thirty years or more. The cattle exhibits were very interesting. I made them all.

The flowers and interior designs for rooms were too grand and involved for me. They were in the hundreds.

In the art display were two little pictures I love. One was a pen-oil sketch of an old log house, a rough board lean-to. The draftmanship was superb. The other was a small oil painting of a mother and her babe. One can only see the infant's shoulders and its head. The eyes are closed and its pink face and little red mouth all puckered, very realistic and natural. All one can see of the mother is her hand holding the baby up, and her face as far down as the nose. Her eyes are closed, too. She is in the act of kissing her baby, in the most beautiful devotion. It is a lovely thing, as fine as any picture of madonnas.

The sheep exhibit was very large. For the first time I saw many of the world's breeds and learned for the first time that about all the pictures of sheep in European art are of these breeds I had never seen before. In my youth I saw Marinos, Hampshires, and possibly Shropshires. The faces of the various breeds of sheep are extremely different. One has a Biblical expression, another a European countenance, etc. The goats are too sophisticated as personalities. They look one in the face and say, "Who the heck are you!" They are too wise.

Rabbits! Hundreds of varieties. They are pathetically passive—too much so for their welfare. Such tolerant creatures. I would rather see them agitated like the bulls and stallions. But they must be true to themselves.

And doves! Hundreds of beautiful varieties, with very picturesque color marking. They were all aliens in captivity, longing for the air. The feathers of their folded wings were pages of a fairy book.

Edna's daughter Christine

The draft horse exhibition was small, and mostly of brood mares and a few colts. There were only two stallions in the show—and they were very inferior in my judgment and memory. The running and saddle horses were another story. They were not all in yet, but still I did not take the time to look them over carefully.

The poultry exhibit was crowded, like the one of cattle. There were representatives of about every breed or strain. The roosters were deceived by the dim light in the building. They thought it was early morning all the time, and kept up a chorus of crowing—B, D, and G flats, and A, C, and E sharps.

From the enormous amounts of beer on the grounds, one would think the Fair was put on by Pabst, Schlitz, Miller High Life, Fox-Head, et al. Those great amounts of beverage somehow make me think of the pig exhibit. We will skip the porcine demonstrations.

Well, let's call it a day at the Fair, Anne. However, there is one more attraction which you must see before we go. On the street in front of the Coliseum is an old silly-faced man. He has a radio going continually, and with a little tin gadget, he plays the most delightful tunes on fly-sprayers, kitchen utensils, toilet plungers, tin horns, shovels, shoes, rubber bands, children's hands and pencils. He keeps up a constant jabber, and his crowd of listeners is so huge that the cops have to herd them out of the street every few minutes. He is effective medicine for the weary, down-hearted, lovesick, unwanted, defeated, hopeless and lonely people who come down the long street.

They stop to listen, forget, and begin anew by laughing. They stand entrapped in the mesh of his nonsense until their legs give out. Finally the cops drive them away again while the old duffer wrinkles up his face and shouts, "Don't do that! Don't drive these good people away." And the cops stop pushing, and the merriment begins anew. The old codger was as lyrically mystifying as a hurdy-gurdy. He made children out of old people, and older people out of children.

Formality, timidity, rigidity, and weariness blew away on the wind till everybody laughed with everybody, and many stood arm in arm or hand in hand. Truly, we were children again! It was there I met two girls about your age from Iowa. And through the old man's good services, we were together for two hours. He made us devoted friends, almost sweethearts. The only mistake I made was not to buy gadgets for all of us. It would have made me a boy again, shoeless, hatless, and full of whistle and song. Such fun we would have had! As it was, I wanted to go back and kiss the chickens, sheep and cows. It was a glorious feeling to be young again. Anne, if you ever see that funny old fellow, don't let him get away. The cops both laughed and cussed at him as he yelled, "Don't! Don't drive them away! They've got money!"

On the bus going downtown I thought of my first visit here. Milwaukee was a big, dark, dirty town then—much of it without electric lights, without pavements, with horses and buggies or wagons. Now, high up and as far as I could see, advertisements burned like glowing branches arranged in block letters with liquid fire running. It made me dizzy and I knew I would pay for the outing. But even now, after more than a week, the longing for the distant years of my childhood from which you and I are separated in time and space, is with me. Like a distant and lost country, it shines and entices on the horizon.

This morning I drove to Waukesha just to get out of the doghouse. It will be a while before I dare attempt a long drive, much as I wanted to come for your birthday. I am always thinking of you, Anne—my darling and most precious! Are you happy? What are you doing these late summer days? Can you mail me just one look at the beautiful valleys from your hill?

It is the only medicine I want. I send you my love.

Uncle Paul

South Survey, Wisconsin
September 21, 1955

Dear Anne:

Today I walked up to the road for the mail. I went up on the hill to read Paul's letter, the one you have just read. In every direction there is a festival of color. The fields are dotted with frost flowers, and on the fences the bittersweet is heavy and just beginning to open. I thought of Paul's little poem, *Summer*, which you like:

With her baggage of yesteryear
And no thought of tomorrow,
She left today
On a train of clouds,
So beautifully gay.

She was up there still today—temperature 76. Looking out of the window of the clouds, she smiled and waved to everyone who had eyes to see her. I waved back and came home along the road where she walked only yesterday.

So now it is autumn. The great upheaval of spring is far away. The sensuousness of summer will soon be forgotten. In the autumn of life, I suppose human beings must be to each other as the kernels of harvest time—even brother and sister, planted as Paul and I are, in the soil of our background. Thus we go on living, capable of yielding happiness and development.

A little while ago, you asked me questions about the "old days." Suddenly, the planning that went into these letters seemed worthwhile, for I want so much to give you a creation that will out-live the manufactures that will delight you tomorrow.

I, too, must thank Paul for taking me to the Fair. But it was a more distant one, I am thinking of now—more fair, since it was one of our first when we were children.

Paul must really have forgotten his varicosities to cover so much ground with you in one day. And how did he get you to view the livestock exhibits? He must have made concessions, promised that you wouldn't go near the races. Why didn't you have your pictures taken in one of those photo stalls? He failed to report some interesting sights: the motley vagabond troupe of all nationalities that people the Midway. Where were my favorite artisans, the glass-blowers? And the jugglers and tumblers and wrestlers and the puppets of the Punch and Judy shows? What an impoverished throng of fair-goers that one old man had to pinch-hit for all of these. But that is what happens when a Fair becomes an advertisement for industry and a display of inventive progress and of breeding and feeding.

Well, I will take you to the Fair, *when we were children*, my first—Paul's third or fourth. Shall we go back? There were no cold and poreless plastics then, nor were there wares of plaster-of-paris and papier-mache. There was real chinaware, the parasols were of silk, and the gay pony whips had leather butts and lashes. There were lovely plumes on sticks and demure and durable kewpie dolls. But best of all was the triple enjoyment . . . First there was that seemingly endless ride when all the world was morning-fresh and the river sparkled as only a fast-moving river does when it is discovered from a hilltop, down among trees with the sun just showing over earth's rim.

This was Anticipation, marred only by the worry that Mamma might forget to give us the extra dollar promised for cleaning the roothouse. My hands were red and rough, and there was grime around the knuckles from washing the jars in well water. There was near-excitement for us when the runaway bay gelding snorted and Papa pointed out two snakes sunning themselves on a rock. He drove a little farther and handed the reins to Mamma and went back.

When he returned, two glossy rattles lay on the large grape leaves in his hand. "Christmas money for you two to spend," he said, "Fifty cents apiece."

Mamma said, so softly I hardly heard, "You probably saved a life, too, John."

On the river bridge the horse flies came in a swarm, and one landed on the belly of the other horse where the whip could not flip it off. Even Papa looked a little scared for a second.

Still there were no jammed-traffic tensions or close-call collisions. By the time we reached Spring Green we were wild with happiness . . .

If the Fair fell short in some respects, the merry-go-round did not. But still it was the Fair—the day I had dreamed of all the long summer!

Homeward-bound, we relived the magic hours and weighed them against the pleasures the others had experienced, and each shared his treasures with the others. We exclaimed over Mamma's wisdom and foresight, for the basket we had been sure was stocked twice too full was empty. In the west a storm was moving in.

Papa stopped the horses, and he and Mamma stood up. Under the front cushion there was a flat box of Wealthy apples. "I am not as smart as your Mother," he said, "This is where the surrey curtains should be. It was such a beautiful clear morning I left them home." He passed us two apples apiece.

Mother said, "If we hurry, dear, we can make the team-shed at the Wyoming Church."

We drove very fast and I was afraid. Very soon the storm hung over us. The lightning came—purifying, terrifying. We reached the horse-shed before the liberating rain.

The expectant calm was like a pause in a symphony before the kettle-drums set in. I covered my eyes, trying hard not to tremble. Paul put his arms around me and held me close. Father handed back the lap-robe with the sea-horse woven in, and I fell asleep with my head on Paul's shoulder . . .

When he woke me, clouds were racing across the moon. All the world that had been so gilt-paper bright, lay black and sodden beside the mouldy hills, and my eyes turned from grand-stands and a carousel out into the twilight to the bare heavens, and then to the barn, sad and forsaken against that leaden sky.

Complaining cows dinned the music of bands from my ears. I was overwhelmed by the misery of just being alive. This was no doubt the first plash of the night-hawks wing in the child-pool of cognizance. There was only the world of reality, and endless longing, and I knew that I would never understand it.

Paul said, "Here are your fan and your plume—you dropped them. Don't cry. Mamma and Papa are tired, too. Tomorrow we'll play Fair. I'll change the teeter-totter into a merry-go-round." And I believed him! This year he didn't even buy you a ride!

I have written this against a background of syncopation and the droning of a disk-jockey's voice. In the room across the hall you are doubtless absorbed with your infinitely important —but

Husband Peter and grandchildren

unnecessary—beauty ritual. This ten o'clock break will bring a program of another generation. If your nail polish is not quite dry, or you are otherwise occupied, I will hear Jerome Kern's theme music about yesterdays.

Do not be saddened by these letters. Most of us are holding the skin of something we had. Other things we have mounted for souvenirs. The "was" and "could have beens" fill our attics. "Is" we never fully accept—"is" the living . . .

Wear *your* gown and mantel of happiness and goodness tomorrow and always, my dear. We love you.

Grandma

The upstairs is very still now and when I turn off the bed lamp the darkness is not total—and traffic will tear the silence.

Suddenly, and irrationally, I am lonesome for the pungency of a lamp blown out . . . And so—I add the inevitable postscript . . .

In this juxtaposition I think the most wonderful words in any language must be *When we were children*. Ever since that time we have lived in and by a succession of happenings—as does a film made of thousands of instantaneous images. And it is in the personal-ness of such happenings that a memory consists. If we but knew why so little of the film retains its clarity the mystery of memory might be solved. But not the lure of yesterdays.

When do we take that first backward look to *when we were children* and find it good—the perfect caption for the constant rewind?

My life bridges the era of great invention and science. I have seen tomorrow unmask each marvel and met the challenge of change simply by living. But one day past summer's thirst finally there was frost. I who had been kin of the weather heard the wind mocking, and searchingly I turned to where the leaf-bells echoed.

Earth alone is faithful, for its beauties are us over whom time keeps endless vigil.

Hired Men
(Sketches and a Conjecture)

"The Death of the Hired Man" first came to my attention during a poetry reading over WHA radio. The reader was Production Manager Raymond Stanley, one of the finest interpreters of poetry in the tradition of Ted Malone, Franklin McCormick, Ken Nordine. We became friends and one of my better poems, "*Snowbound* Rebroadcast" is a memorial to him.

Robert Frost described so well the plight of his subject that one questions if it ever need be done again. Still, the subject may stand illumination in a more general way, because soon there will be no one to tell the story of those once-upon-a-time wanderers.

Theirs was not often a pleasant existence. There were practically no tenant houses where, as today, the farm employee may live with his wife and children, or as an itinerant. Neither was there any form of welfare or Social Security, and if they were a mite strange, retarded or even handicapped, they covered this carefully lest they be institutionalized. Many were required to sleep in an outbuilding or the barn. If there was a ghetto in rural America, it was in the status and lifestyle of the hired man. Worse yet, most of them belonged nowhere. They came and they went, the real Ishmaels in that era of our history.

Though they are gone now, most of them deceased, they can be sought out, their time with us relived. For one who has known uninterrupted aloneness, it is easy to keep appointments with the loneliness in others.

And here I digress, for this must be said: From early childhood until five years ago, when the last departed this world, I always had close friends in the priesthood—another segment of our society that bears a special mark, often having shallow roots in this world. Of these people, Pere Lacordaire wrote in his "Tribute:"

> To teach and pardon, to console and bless;
> To share suffering and penetrate all secrets;
> To be a member of each family, *yet belonging to none.*

And writers, yes. A lonely lot, mostly. August Derleth, in a joyous moment, suddenly apprehensive over human brevity, laughter and tears turned to salt, could say to me, "How else endure the loneliness that's life!"

Once, when I shied away from a clergy-friend's compliment about the warmth in our home, he said, "You should know: Truth is Humility." In that spirit it may be admitted that the hired men's lives were better than average with us, that a conscious effort was to make them feel "at home," to dispel the internecine atmosphere of "outsider."

The stories I give you have little to do with sequential recall. They are chosen for their exposition of kind, and are genuine, though, for obvious reasons, most have fictitious names. None of these characters are representative of the vacation high-schoolers, young fellows needing to earn money for wheels or whatever. Mostly the latter moved on to full or normal lives.

Austin Marley: He was the first, when we lived on Pleasant Ridge. He was from England, a victim of shell-shock, from which he had not recovered. He was very smart and overly emotional. Strange things could trigger moods of despondency, such as fields of dandelions in bloom. Crying toddlers upset him, and since we had two and a baby expected in mid-July, I was not sorry to see him move on to work for childless neighbors.

Kyle: Had been a western cowpoke. He was a goodlooking, mouthy chap who wanted to address me only as "Cookie." I remember him vividly on a chilly April morning when he, feigning illness, asked my father-in-law, whose upstairs room was across from his, to have me bring him some hot water and soda. When I brought it, he was lying on top of the covers, naked as a water snake, *ready*. . . .

There have been too many bad jokes about the hired man and the farmer's daughter; almost none about "crushes" on the farmer's wife. The latter was probably more common than the former. Was he fired? No, Kyle was the most popular with the menfolk of all our helpers. But I had the Aquarius Sign on him, and he quit calling me "Cookie."

Mattie: Was illegitimate, one who, because of an abusive environment, wore his bastardy like a scarlet letter. He liked, above all, the task of driving me to town for grocery shopping, of being seen with me. He was an honest person, a hard worker, and it grieved me that such small incidents added, in his mind, to stature. Association with Mattie influenced a related decision that came years later. We could not afford all-winter help, and so such men moved on to other jobs.

True, several of the men came back after a few years to work for us again. Mattie was one such. But between Mattie and the next man, there was a kind of post-Depression parade of parolees and knights-of-the-road. Fibber McGee and Mollie's closet would run a poor second with the contents of our attic. Added to generations of family clutter are many newspaper articles originally clipped by these unfortunate souls. And what an exhumation there will be someday!

Carl: World War II was beginning in Europe. He was a bright, cynical, middle-aged man. He was a radio buff and said he'd work "reasonable enough if I can listen to radio evenings and on Saturday afternoons?" And, he added, "Sundays off?"

I had acquired the habit of listening to Milton Cross's broadcasts from the Metropolitan Opera during that Saturday time slot, but many considerations had priority over a farm woman's whim. Carl had a proprietary manner, the only such hired man we ever had. Soon as the noon meal was over, he would go to the living room, turn on the radio and settle himself in the most comfortable chair. Though the program he wanted to hear usually was an hour away, not once did he carry a dish to the kitchen as a courtesy to me.

The program was a Marine Band Concert, broadcast from Washington D.C. It was a fine program, which I enjoyed as much as if it had been the opera. It took several weeks before the radio announcer's introduction and sign-off words penetrated my consciousness. The conductor had the same name as Carl's, with "Jr." tacked on. "Yes," he said, "he's the eldest of my five children." Then he offered a bit more of his background.

He and his wife had run a truck garden on Long Island, and had processed some of their products, such as sweet gherkin pickles. They had divorced. Why this happened, I did not enquire. When the concert was over, he went to his room until suppertime. Then his preference (and ours) was Lucky Strike's "Your Hit Parade."

Sundays were spent in bed in his room with a pint of good bourbon (he was never drunk) and girlie magazines—"Silk Stocking" being one of these.

Earlier, I used a sixty-five dollar word: *internecine.* I was thinking of Carl when it came to mind. I could not like him —given to disparaging remarks, not so much *what* but *how* said: "Wherever you have women, you have hair."

We were nearing the 1940s and he read the newspapers avidly. Any rumors about involvement with war pleased him. "If we can get into the war, we'll have prosperity again. It will be real good for the country," was a frequent comment. My son, who would go off three years later, was fifteen.

Lauren was one of those who contributed to our national prosperity. He did so by falling at Ardennes Forest in the Battle of the Bulge, and was one of the inspirations for a poem, "Dream Memories of a Hired Man."

The other casualty was Edward, a neighbor lad who went to the first "War to end all wars" in 1917. His fate was felt the more keenly because the Armistice bells were about to ring out, and this brought home to us the terrible trenches and the tales of atrocities.

My sons all had "Edward" for their middle names, and they were given without any notion why until years later. The realization came about when a tactless woman read one of their obituaries. She asked, "Why ever did you give them the same middle names? Didn't you know it's bad luck? That he would die young?"

One endures such incidents. I knew the remark was her superstition. But the wound made by her assertion was slow closing and I demanded of myself a reason—such was my vulnerability.

And the original Edward emerged from the memory-cave. I was nearly twelve and he came to say good-bye, and leaving, he kissed me. The first kiss from a young man! I felt guilty for having forgotten him that long.

His memory was there when the word came about Lauren. Soon after he came to us, his family moved to the northern part of Wisconsin. He was with us nearly two years and was one of my favorites.

We sent subscriptions to *Reader's Digest* to our son and a couple of other servicemen. It was that company that sent us the message along with a small refund check. Then the poem was waiting in the wings.

Herbie was a mildly retarded, dear little fellow, who loved pretty things. If the meal was not on the table when the men came in (during the planting and harvest seasons, a cardinal sin of which I was often guilty), he'd move his chair in front of one of the china cupboards and sit there admiring the dishes and trinkets. He seemed neither young nor old.

When I think of him, I remember an expectant look on his face. He has brought another bouquet of wildflowers, and is waiting for the little hug across his shoulders—from me. He was full of concern, lifting and carrying, saying such made-up words as, "It's mighty *suffoc*" (for hot and humid). Or if rain threatened, he'd advise, "Better take your *umbersol*!" Herbie should be in heaven.

Charlie could have been the original for "Bathless Grogan," who years later was to make his appearance in the "Li'l Abner" comic strip. If, in the three months he was at our place, he ever bathed, it was top secret. Instead of washing, he doused himself liberally with Old Spice cologne. To this day, that popular fragrance makes me nauseous—maybe because I was pregnant at that time and the senses are often affected.

He, too, had an every-Sunday pastime: the stock car races. Early each Sunday morning, he was off to wherever it was the races were held. Gloriously, he was back by six o'clock, because if he had not been, I would have had to help with the evening milking. Usually I greeted him with, "Well did you have a good time today?"

I found his consistent response, "Nope. Nobody got kilt!" hilarious until one day a driver was killed. Then I guessed that Charlie had been born a century too late. He might have enjoyed the spectator sport of lynching.

Russell was another who was nearing middle age. He was an uncommonly handsome Irishman, wasted by chronic alcoholism. Sober, he was witty, companionable and a splendid workman. But he chose the most inopportune times for his sprees, such as during planting or harvesting season. These could last half a week. Upon returning, he too had a stock pronouncement—"Ah, good liquor never hurt anyone."

Tension in Peter was mounting fast on that last Sunday when he came back after three days' "vacation." He showed me a badly-swollen wrist and forearm, and asked for the rubbing alcohol. Thanking me, he took the bottle out onto the front porch.

I should have known better had the Sunday dinner not been at a crucial stage. During Russell's sojourn I kept everything alcoholic, vanilla and lemon extracts, for instance, in a box under my bed. When I went to call him to dinner the bottle was empty and Russell nowhere in sight. Soon we heard him in his upstairs room, moving about like a caged animal.

"Let the so-and-so croak," Peter said, justly disgusted. But Father Dan had just arrived, after substitute parish service. He took this poor unfortunate to a nearby hospital, where his stomach had to be pumped.

Years later, coming from one of those bouts, he fell into a shallow creek and drowned. A mutual lawyer friend, Dan McKinley, reminded us: "It wasn't the liquor that killed Russell. It was water!" He was right!

Lucas, for want of a better, is my name for this fortyish man. He arrived one evening wearing new tennis shoes. He was well-dressed and had only one change of clothes, in a paper bag, with him. He came close to nightfall, on the day after the suspected murder of Evelyn Hartley in La Crosse.

He said he'd work only if he could be paid in cash at the end of each week. His speech was refined and he moved with a peculiar quickness and grace. "The fastest worker we've ever had," was Peter's verdict on the second day.

His room was above mine and around 3:30 each morning he was up, pacing back and forth. He'd watch for the mail and as soon as it was in the box, he got in his car and drove to the road, where he'd stay long enough to have perused the newspaper before bringing the mail to the house. His meals were eaten fast, then he went to listen to his car radio.

In the Evelyn Hartley case, quite a little was made about a tennis shoe outside the basement window through which she'd been abducted. Did I dare share my unfounded suspicion with Peter, who was brusque and forthright?

My feelings surfaced on the sixth day. I'd loitered at grocery shopping and suddenly realized that the school bus would be dropping our daughter off. I became so frantic, loading the groceries and urging Peter over and over to drive faster, that I had to explain my fears. Panic increased as I noted that Peter did not find these suspicions as wild as I'd supposed he might. He shared the apprehension, and we literally flew over the road, arriving at the same time as the bus at the top of our long driveway.

All was well, for the time being. Lucas was on the machine shed roof, nailing down loose tin. But at supper I knew I should have kept the matter to myself. Peter began questioning him. "Where are you from? Where did you work before coming here?"

The man gave courteous answers but he was uneasy and when, as usual, he hurried outside, I warned Peter to knock off the third degree, and I told him I'd brought home the cash with which to pay Lucas. This was done, as agreed upon. He went to bed at the usual time. In the morning he was gone.

It was all circumstantial and slight to boot. So why this lingering distrust? Would I handle it differently today? Talk to the police? Tell them what? That a troubled, reticent man was working for us, that I who am not cowardly had been terribly afraid? Now this seems long ago and far away. Evelyn Hartley's murderer may also be dead.

Nine hired men, to give you a sense of how our life went. I tried to be kind, to see to their well-being: good food, clean beds and clothes. Recording Angel, put that in your book. But I did not love them, as the Bible admonishes.

Part III
The Kristin Poems

More than Twice-Told Tales

The Valley

A pastoral prototype
it hid unanythings never to be named:
evening emanations from ravine and wood,
mists, a sometimes wedgewood bowl—
by turns harebell to gentian blue,
its darknesses no better lit
by lantern than firefly,
dawns coming on like water over quicksand.

This was my valley, cored with solitude,
where inself was for gathering armfuls
like wildflower and fruit.
Death was neighbor there,
to talk with on river bank,
over rattlesnakes on rock, through woods
that hid the human and beastly from hunters,
and where I once had with him
a rendezvous we did not keep;
and in other peril, like St. Paul's,
I lay half underneath my father while tornado and flood
robbed us of all but life.
There was neighbor death, suspect,
never to be let known I was afraid—except,
except when Frances rose
from firelight of long evening talk.

Leaves from Family Trees

The uncles, four Bohemians, black of beard,
were Antaeus-tall. They came to visit Baba, "Little
Mother,"
though attention centered on my own.
Their brother, my father, John,
had gotten himself a handsome Dane.
After that no valley could have been the same.
"The four apostles," she called them—
this Freyja full of tease and fire—
merrymakers, which Papa was not.
He sat with Baba, to one side,
listening, warmed by their wit; she was at times
as if for the first hearing of it,
or she was somewhere else with loved ones
who never change. (In williwaws of memory,
Baba wore her widow's weeds thirty years,
ruffled bonnets and rosary beads.)
Oh I would not ever be that old!
or cross, like Mama, with her for knitting a second foot
onto the heel-holes of our stockings.

Uncle Lew was first to bring Frances into view
with: "Twenty years today since she took sick. . . ."
Outside, the valley forces made Allhallows wind
a dirge; evil spirits hissed from green wood on the
hearth,
and in my father's eyes the same void as Baba's had—
wherein a child looks far and deep as *never.*

Once on a Country Road

Papa fetched the box and got a picture out:
"Frances was shy, always wanting to be clean—those days
that wasn't easy, the house too small, all us boys. . . ."
It was Paul who grasped the memory ring (I held the photo).
"We had the walled spring, cool in summer, autumn cold,
in winter warm. She took her Sunday clothes,
a clean old petticoat for towel. The sun was hardly up."
"She washed her hair, I scolded," Baba said.
"A girl fourteen must never take a chill."
Then Paul again: "Her teeth were chattering, but she laughed,
shaking out her long hair like two black wings,
and saying: 'The sun will dry it on the way to town.' "
"That would be several hours' ride," another uncle said,
"October days are short." "It was the *moon*,"
Baba muttered, "*the time of month*."
They rode silent on a carousel I wanted so to see
I held the picture Frances closer to the lamp.
—I see her better now the inner lights are on,
and though the photo fades, a modal music lingers:

It was her birthday. The older brothers worked out
in summer, but before woodcutting time they were at home.
Their gift of money was for a picture to be taken, and Paul,
sixteen, who had no wages, would drive her into town
where a studio had opened—a trip never to be forgotten:
frost was late and autumn long that year, the trees
were almost bare, and when they reached the Ridge
as far as eye could travel, hills rolled into hills,

the Mounds Madonna blue, Michaelmas daisies
everywhere in bloom, and between the wagon wheels
the beard grass flattened like fur. Paul said,
"She watched the zigzags of wild geese out of sight,
as if it were the last look she'd ever have of these . . .
her eyes too bright. Later, the photo-artist thought
she was the prettiest. Roses in her cheeks that high!"
They ate their lunch, and when supplies were bought
he gave her leftover pocket silver for a length of calico.
"When she kissed me on the cheek I thought her face
too hot."
—She chose a black with yellow dots.

The journey home was not so hard. The hills
they had to climb would now be going down. At first
they talked and made up songs. When it was dark at
five
he no longer gave the horses rein. Around Frances,
asleep,
he put his arm and thought again how warm she was.
The night sounds a farm boy knows and likes
filled him with sadness and a kind of fear:
"There must have been a dozen owls about.
Leaves caught on tall weeds whispered in the wind,
a wildcat quarrel, foxes yipping, sheep and cowbell,
dogs were barking, and nowhere a single sign of light.
So dark it was! But then the moon came up."
—I seldom saw it over Pleasant Ridge through any other
eyes:
red diffusion of sky that went from tangerine
into chartreuse, then moonrise a balanced ball
between the sea lion hills, while just ahead
our valley, an ocean darkness, yawned.
The rustlings took on shape and he was glad she woke,
until the lines were in her quick hands, the horses pulled

to stop beside the road. She asked him then:
"Where are all the wagons going? Is it a funeral?
We have to let them pass." He flicked the team
with his hickory whip and got the reins again,
the wagon onto the wheel tracks. In the flaming
moonlight
she stood and pointed: "Don't you see? The Bradleys-
Adamses—
Baba with Mr. and Mrs. Egan like when Papa died.
Why?
Her face is covered. I see you! Why are you crying,
Paul?"
He shook her then to make her sit, and said
he was right there, but she went on naming people
in the ghostly cortege. "My head hurts," she said.
They had come to the rim above their valley.
Paul released a brake and the pushed team
went galloping down the familiar ground
as he held her, kneeling in the wagon box.

Three days she fought in fever, frightening them
with talk. While Indian Summer spent itself
her brothers brought coolness every hour from the
spring.
The married sisters came, and Baba prayed and aged.
My father went horseback thirty miles
for medicine too late to give.

Frances: Fears That Pinch the Breastbone

Who were you, Frances,
thresholding womanhood one distant fall!
Keeper of secrets, essence of dusk,
your lean and level gaze
weighs me: weights in an abundant,
leaden life. Unschooled seventh child,
illusiveness looked into the dry plate
Allhallows Day, your fourteenth year,
with honesty and ineffable beauty
mantling you plainly as the massed hair
in fever tendrils, ribbon held.
That brow (when brows were decent to expose)
and bearing could have modeled caryatids.
Who, lovely Frances, arranged you so,
the pose forever classic—a doomed Cassandra?
Dear girl, they would have burned you once
for witch, or put you in a snake pit—
had you lived.

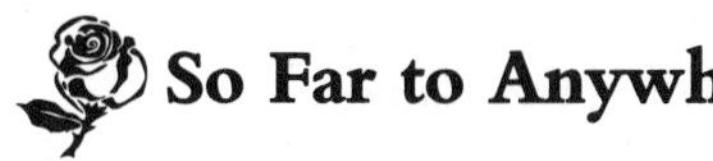

So Far to Anywhere

1. Forebears

Proscenium altered, props and costumes gone,
the dramas fade. From the cast of that time
to mine, snatches of dialogue return because
I am a listener.

None can describe the Valley between central
and western prongs of trident hills in 1871.
Ignatius Kryz brought to his purchased land
two Marys (wife and daughter), Lewis, Anna, Frank,
Emmaline, and John. Stones walled the small tomb
of Anthony, left in Bohemia near Sumava Forest.

Off the Baltic Sea on the farthest inlet
of Vejle Fjord a sheltered city lay, even then
striped with railroad and cables. There, nineteen
years Kristin Nielsen grew learning Danish skills
and arts she would take to America. The next six
Chicago knew her charm and beauty, challenged
her industry, and wit in avoiding ambush—
till Father came to the Fair.*

She told of their coming to Wyoming Valley:
"His brother Paul was waiting at the depot.
We loaded our belongings in the lumber wagon,
began a trip I'll not forget. At first romantic,
bobbing on the spring seat between such men,
I thought, 'Out here John is all mine.
Nellie will never get to see him again!'

*Columbian exposition

We came to the Wisconsin River—
it was like a Constable done violence by Van Gogh.
After the river willows and Hillside Colony
we crossed over a ridge of birches and pines,
went into the density of oak-clad bluffs.
Shrouding fog fell, as darkness rose like a tide
that last September of the century."

She knew it a Limbo and all the way stations to Eden:
Valley sounds and silence testing sanity,
its frozen sulks, erratic winds and warmth
their mettle. The unsaddled creek was melody
till vernal equinox, 1902, flooded its banks:
Her time had come—frightened and far from kin—
labor too long for a heart congenitally weak,
the boy over-large for bones misshapen to wasp-waist.
She was never fully well again.

2. Gift of Life

Pre-Christmas, 1905, friends coming from Chicago!
Son Leo, almost four, hooked tugs to whiffletrees
and driving to town held the horses' lines—
ultimate achievement! For his parents,
company joy, freedom of laughter made continence
a casualty: The end of January she was sure.

Soapstone warmed, in layers of blankets they rode
in a sledge box to a farther town. She said,
"Your God-haunted father could compromise.
He loved me enough. But I was raised on dogmatism.
No Valkyrie, I knew myself a wicked coward—

"Doctor Reese heard us out, examined me, confirmed
what I knew, seemed willing to abet us.

We were to come back within two months.
He made up the prescription himself."

She was showing-with-child when spring came to
 equinox.
Leo was scrubbed and trimmed for a birthday
 photograph,
herself for a second visit to Doctor Reese.
Greeting them he offered neither apology nor surprise,
but asked if they had an orchard? had they ever tried
to shake small green apples from a tree?

He got a book from his desk, opened it, explaining,
to pictures of how the placenta is attached.
"He put his arm around me." Mother repeated his
 words:
"'I gave you no ergot, only a tonic. Do not worry.
I'll be there to take good care of you. Trust me!' "

She was on her knees washing floors when he came
uncalled the fourteenth of September, saying:
"Something fine must happen on this day
that honors the Cross. Besides, the moon is full."
She gave him a pastry and made fresh coffee.
When he went to where Father was fencing,
she chased and caught a spring rooster for their meal,
and felt the first stress of unsealing.

3. Fulcrum

Young I came to wish she had not purged
conscience, telling too soon her childbed fears.
I was loved. What else mattered then?

What matters now is a kind of knowledge
that gives tangential strength, a circular
view, an advantage over those who would
role-play God with the unborn.

I had thought to stay aloof from issues
of legality and amorality until her namesake
said, "I went before the State Legislature.
I was articulate and made them understand
a woman has rights over her own body.
You would have been proud of me."

Proud, no. Tried was the locked gate
to my opinions. Facing an exercise in sorts
of relatives—blood and philosophy—
it was as a scales: In one was desperation
to live; the other searching for a cause,
and victim of today's dictum to be heard.

I would be neither balance nor fulcrum for psyche
though placed as daughter and mother between
mother and daughter.   We are all revelation,
our insights of the Holy Spirit.

4. *The Tinder Box (for Leo)*

Cell by cell that which makes you earliest memory
is moving out. In this hospital room we recall
our sibling past like tired swimmers afraid
beyond the breakers. Where you searched a beacon
I knew piranha lurk. Now my hand
on your drumskull evokes recognition. I bend
to your calcinized ear: *Leo? Vaya con Dios.*

To Cheyne-Stokes rhythm I pray journey's end.
Its log hangs at your feet,
a leftover page like end paper to atlas.
I remove it, begin: *To my brother, Address unknown:*
Remember Doctor Reese saying, "Edna is three.
Meningitis or not, she walks. Now or never!"
Home, I trembled at core of our Triangulum:
Mother and Father were far as Andromeda and Aries,
but you its *C* toward whom I stilted to safety.
"Now can I take her fishing?" you asked
with eight-year-old acumen. "F i s h i n g?" I whined,
muscle pains and tensions released. Mother scolding:
"Go do you chores. You've made her cry." I clung,
but went with her to the castered chair.

The inside-outside woodbox was as miles and miles
from dining room through kitchen. I listened
for *Clop!* of its outer lid against the housewall,
for thudding armloads that would later go
into mica-windowed and cooking stoves.
On cue the inner lid moved. To satisfy half
my short lifetime's goal I could surmount fear
to exercise newfound freedom of limping to grasp
the woodbox edge and coax: "Kitty? kitty-kitty-kitty."
Claws and nose, teeth like ivory combs, whiskers,
golden eyes pulled slantwise by the wooden weight,
she issued past me a Minerva: fullblown Maltese
to the tip of her tail.
Father said, "That clever cat!
Imagine her raising both covers to get in here!"

Your form punctuated doorway sky, snowy, pinched,
saying, "Look, little sister's eyes are big as saucers."
We felt zero blasts of anger/air as Mother said,
"How dare you say she looks like a dog? Close the door.

You think we don't know who put kitty in the
 woodbox?"
Could I turn back to tell by unspoken hurt
for your sad knowing it would be useless to answer.
(I did go with you in spirit taking the cat outside.)

Your eleventh natal day in March Uncle Soren
in Denmark sent ANDERSEN'S FAIRY TALES.
From our sparsely peopled valley we outstripped
Jules Verne by forty days as you became sundry princes,
mole, swineherd, Ole Luckoie; assigning me the roles
of Helga, Little Match and the other girls. *The Tinder
 Box*
was near the end. I hear your uneven reading still,
the horrid witch telling the young soldier
what is beneath the hollow tree, of the hundred lamps
burning there: "Then you will see three doors, you can
open them, keys are in the locks. Entering the first
you will find at the center of the room a great chest;
a Dog is seated on it, *his eyes are large as saucers*."
As of one mind our eyes met. We understood, in silence
saw another guarded door without its key to Why
our mother loved you less who loved her best.

Indexed years: Our Ides of March—September days
fell page on page. We paid the usual human debts
for Oedipus-urge that influence choice of mate.
Obeisant to twin masters of Injury and Pride, dialog
decreased, from separate Gehennas we dared peer
through the crumbling chimney of life, impervious
to tindered grievances flaring hot.

Like jetsam our lately conversations surface:
Do we carry from birth the runaway cell
as poisonous flower foretells the fatal berry?
Have we been here before? Those other April-endings
(always in April): Ignatius, Lewis, Frank, Paul,
our father, all as you were fuel and furnace both.

My brother, release the freedom-fanning draught!
With first and faltering steps join an ever-
widening arc of Light. Return this night
to the dream from which we die when we are born
so far from anywhere.

September 13, 1909

Tomorrow she will be three. Kristin sits beside
a window that is open on an ornate porch
where kittens wrestle in a leapfrogging race.
Saffron, her special pet, almost always wins.
Watching them she does not understand why
she no longer hurts seeing other young at play.
A child accepts, unknowing that the years
will tell more of righteous envy, anger, pain.

From the railing, half-hidden by trumpet vines,
a tortoise-shell stranger pounces on her favorite:
Nasturtium paws comb summer air as geysers spurt.
With bared teeth the killer tomcat waits
until the kitten is still, before he feeds.
Vocal chords useless now as her legs, no sounds
will come, while a hammer pounds inside her chest
and head to take all breath, and mark for life
in her a sadness for small deaths.
Father lowers
his newspaper, hearing her in gasping shock.

Outdoors, he says, "Your heart!" pressing his hand
against her ribs as if to keep it in its cage:
"What we are feeling is your heartbeat."
In his arms, on his lap, her muffled sobs begin.
"A heart tells us when to be glad, afraid or sad.
It will say when you are brave enough to take steps."
Satin brow scraping his collarbone, she whispers,
"I can hear your heart," thinks it must be like
the golden moon that goes back and forth
in their teller of time, or like a windmill
that pushes down to bring water up.

Next day, after the birthday-candled cake, Kristin calls
on her heart, hearing its clock sounds setting the pace—
a pump, stroking over and over: YOU CAN   YOU
      CAN   YOU CAN
until she steps and falls, steps and falls . . . and walks.

First Journey

I

The team was slow
as logs move,
and a woman drove them,
countenance a barren field
when she looked at her husband
lying in the wagon.

The child faced forward—
a Thing was with Papa back there,
like forgetting;
it crawled her meadow mind, nameless
as the fear he might never be a warm lap again.
Doré angels adorned the cover
of the Picture Bible she clutched,
and over the riverland
came a sound of trumpeting.
Mother spoke to God, and lashed the horses,
and though he groaned
the child would not look back.

Across the sky where distant bluffs
lay like animals in her Book
a snake was moving.
Dampness rolled with the river
that October time of early dusks
when they met the train,
hissing underneath and writhing smoke,
lynx' eyes and kinds of owl talk,
this, into which they must go,
"If your father is to be mended," Mother said.
(He the giant who made trees fall,
magician who changed her to princess.)
She went quaking behind the litter,

small for the blinding vision
that fear is hating all one does not understand.

Falling timber crushes more than bones,
a Thing is given name, becomes an indecision.
It hovered like a hawk over the hospital—
while his child made friends;
One, whose presence lighted that continent
of strange mothers and fathers, of new shapes and noise,
knew she would like the garden
where clustered berries grew on trees,
and on bushes such tiny apples.
Reaching for these she cried with sudden pain.
The chaplain thought of thorns and spread her fingers,
but she raised her dress to show him
how a strained garter bent the fastening pin
that tore a four-year's tender thigh.
Unhooking the tabs he turned her stocking down,
then up the stairs, hand-in-hand, they ran,
two children looking for Sister to tend the wound.

They met her mother, who saw
only the garter, looped over a suspect-stranger's thumb,
and the guilty blood on a little girl's leg.
Hearing a woman's anger out, the friend turned away—
in his eyes another Thing the child was never to forget.

The hawk went home to its clouds,
and her father drove the horses
clopity-clop over the frozen ground—
yet somewhere it circled still.

II

Grow, child! Accept loss,
come to terms with shamed innocence, and injustice,
take up position in council, and battlement,
become sum total of all that was,
with mind a Potter's Field over which memory glides
like night birds, searching the infinitesimal.

Forget where you came at sun
and savored the tears of loves begun,
but linger where the far away rhythm
of hooves and riverwash and early owl
counterpoints a luminous spiritual
of mountain ash and appled hawthorn.
Treasure all that ramparts the knowing heart,
and gives eyes for backs of mirrors,
and ears deaf to defilement;
a tongue with delicacy for truth.

The Christening Picture

"Waters of Baptism may help her overcome fear."
Kristin trembles hearing them: "Baptism?"
Do they mean trying to teach her to swim again?
"You made plans twice before," her father says,
"then allowed neither minister to follow through."
"They said Baptism is not necessary to salvation."
"Does that matter? They are good men," he reasons.
Her mother's lips double-underscore that it does!

A far place is where the godparents-to-be live,
also the priest of her father's faith who agrees
that uncleansed souls must linger in Limbo
forever thirsting after Christian rebirth.

Arrangements finished, Kristen is giddy with relief
at finding only the church, no river in sight.
First there is Mass and then sacramentals are readied.
Hollow inside she thinks about the christening dinner.

Father Ambauem, taken with her owlish solemnity,
pours the water too generously over corkscrew curls
and releases a tears-sluice that cannot be stoppered.
Finally he lifts her in vested arms: "Dear child,
why are you crying so hard?" She searches his eyes,
not yet having a glib answer for every Why.
He gives her a coin, repeats the question, adds,
"I'd like to know for a book I'm writing?"
The nameless fear too layered for revealing, she says,
"I am going to have a picture taken." It is not enough.
"You've spoiled my curls." On her feet again she hears
his comment, abashed by their shared amusement.
Clenching her first silver dollar, she banks the remark
to withdraw with interest years later when reading

from WINGED WORDS his dissertation of
ECCLESIASTES
"Vanity of vanities and all is vanity."

The Turtle

After a Sunday picnic beside the river
Tomorrow shines in on Kristin waking to say:
"I'm not four anymore!" Her birthday dress and shoes
are on the cedar chest. Downstairs the table is set
for breakfast with a china bowl in the center,
net covered. Kristin, thinking it holds fresh berries,
stands on a chair, sees pebbles, leaves, a sardine can
of water. One leaf moves to another! Alive!
The spotted green turtle found by brother Leo!
A bright day dissolves in her fear of things that crawl.

Weeks that follow shine on neither her nor turtle:
She wishing it dead in the leaky granite pan
provided by Leo, obsessed with its welfare.
"I boiled this dish," their mother says, spooning salad
from the china bowl, "so it's clean as when new."
Kristin goes outside to gag and think, determines
she would rather starve and make them sorry for her.

Near summer's end the strange pet plods about the
house—
"Be careful where you step!" has become a cliche.
When school opens Leo reads all about box turtles
trying in vain to have Kristin hold it while he
points out the horny plates that join at the edges,
each with ridges around: "The 'Cyclopedia
says these are like tree rings for telling turtle's age.
Ours is three years old." Father adds, "About a month
and you children can fix a place with dirt and leaves
where it will sleep all winter in the root cellar."

It is back for Easter, uglier than ever,
staring at Kristin with lidless reptilian eyes,

its head doing an alphabet of sign language
(Cousin Wilma is deaf-mute.) making mean *Hi ii ss es*
"I will make believe it died," she lies to herself,
but next day Leo is angry, catching her cat
greedily licking butter off the turtle's back.
"A dirty trick!" he says, "I ought to tell on you."

That evening their mother examines the tortoise,
showing them how tightly it can close its armor,
how legs must be spread for straddling the bottom shell.
"My brothers in Denmark had one for many years.
Theirs got big," she says, leaning back to let it walk
up her dress front. Leo kneels to better observe:
"It lifts one foot at a time to keep its balance."
Teasing, Mother says, "It could be worn for breastpin!"
Kristin leaves them to think about what must be done.

Autumn, the creature has been people-imprinted,
waits on Leo's bare feet until taken on his lap.
When he is not there it tries to climb Kristin's leg.
She becomes a nutmeg grater of gosling bumps,
fine body hair stands at attention even when
sitting cross-legged on chairs. She is admonished:
"Little girls who expect to grow up as ladies
do not sit so!—like Indian and Chinese men!"

Doomsday! Holding the turtle against Kristen's braids,
Mother says What a pretty barrette it would make.
Breastpin? Barrette? She considers running away.
When her mother goes to feed and water chickens
Kristin finds the turtle in a patch of sunset.
Deprived of caution, instinct forfeited for trust,
enjoying the warmth, head outward its eyes are closed.
She puts one foot with full weight on the carapace
and waits, afraid to look but with small sense of guilt.

Its head hanging like a prune, she hides the dead thing
under a cupboard as Leo comes in from school.

As after any violent storm there comes the calm.
Faced with her crime, Kristin does not lie but departs
their company for silence her father respects:
"Little one, tell me why? That—nothing more—Why?"
"It was getting big. Mama wanted a breastpin."
(His finger threatens.) "Everything dies—it had to—"
said, she seals her mouth, intercepting an exchange
between them: "Mother no longer shocked, a sadness
in him: "The difference is you *killed* the turtle."
A tigress defends herself: "You killed the steer, pigs
and lambs I played with, my friends the roosters."
Mother says, "For our food. Turtle was Leo's pet!"
Warily, as if he knows, comes her father's 'Explain."
Knowing importance of reasons when reasons must be
    had
she throws herself against him, sobbing fearfully:
"Every time we go to church I look at the Virgin's
    statue
with her one foot crushing the serpent's head."

The Shaving Mug

Kristin soon to be seven, is loving and sad
for having no gift for the one most dear.

To swish of wind's invisible attire she slips
away to look for a bee tree. The woods exude
aromatics as she struggles through underbrush,
comes to rattlers sunning on a flat rock.
Honeybee tree forgotten she finds a stout stick,
thinking only of the bounty that will be paid.

Back to the ridge field where her father
is harvesting grain: "I would like to borrow
your pocket knife, opened." She adds, "Please."
"What do you want with it? and the sharp blade—
suppose you should stumble?" (The lameness again!)
She says crisply, "To cut the rattles off my snakes."

They approach the rock. Her small importance dims
at the stern look of him: "Show me the stick you used!"
He measures it twice against each strung-out rattler.
"Do you understand that they could have struck
full length? Death has passed you by this day!" Unlike
her prey, pride will turn bellyside up before sundown:
"But they were scared of me! Some crawled away."
Her father is kneeling now, his hands gripping her arms
are warm but the voice is ice, "How many? And
where?"
"Three or more went back into the crevice."
His head is bowed. He speaks with God.
She touches his hair, "Father?" never having named
him so before, "Will you cut off their tails?"

He hands them to her on a mullein leaf, points
to the largest, "Thirteen rattles. It was twice

your age. What else have you to say for yourself?"
"I went out to find a honey tree for your birthday.
Now there's bounty money. I've seen a shaving mug."
Lifted in his arms she studies the deep anguished eyes
for her first cognition of love's terrible bondage.

The Wall Sampler

Her mother closes the Bible and says happily,
"So Abraham didn't have to kill his only son."
Kristin, sick of Jehovah, wonders how bad is Satan
but whom can she ask, since she was slapped
for saying out loud that God was mean to send bears
out of the forest to tear forty little boys apart
just for calling old Eliseus a "Bald head."
It won't help any to hide the Good Book again.

Outside she joins her father in the orchard
digging a hole for the calf already like Lazarus.
Under the spiraea bushes a tunnel is formed
that serves Kristin for winnowing unpopular
opinions: angers about Lot and his wife,
prophets, the Israelite passage of the Red Sea.
Lately she has taken to talking to herself,
"It's not fair. Only clean and nice things like trees,
flowers, sweet wood smoke rise up to where God is,
and all that's not goes into the ground where devils
live."
(She forgets about the rain.) Seeing Shep lift his hind leg
beside the grindstone she feels simultaneously
the urge and rebellion. "I will do it," she says.
Back of and against the machine shed Kristin stands
on her head to force an unusual hotspring.
Feet on the grass again, expecting bears she stares
at the wooded hills but only some blue bottle flies
worry her long hair, warm and smelly wet.
Mama!
If her mother sees she will have to tell her wicked act.
Father!
He can save her from spankings but she is ashamed
to be seen like this. Hiding in the murky shed
she spots Leo's twine fishnet hanging from a peg.

Hurriedly back from the creek to where her father
is laying sod back over the hole, crocodile tears,
and dress dripping wet, she gasps, "I went fishing
and fell in." (That much is true, having flung herself
in the shallow water.) He has that worried look again:
"Never go fishing alone. You're only seven."
He gathers her up, net, shovel and the other tools.

In dry clothes sitting beside him at the kitchen table
with cookies and buttermilk, she listens to his words:
"Snakes, caves, poison ivy. Now the creek! What's
next?"
She knows she has handled the situation well,
promises too easily, "I will be more careful."
But she avoids his eyes for within range of hers
falls the wall sampler:

THE WAGES
OF SIN IS DEATH!

A matter for the spiraea tunnel!

N.B. Spiraea is the bridal wreath bush.

Endings to Be Remembered

for Margaret Holley—rural school teacher

Black and white turned beige, the photo projects
a study in contrasts: The schoolhouse peeling paint,
you standing beside Gyneth and Edith, Flossie and
Marie,
with a dozen sad-faced others in front, third-grade Niels
already a testimonial (Today a reprimand?)
to our mothers' Danish dishes.
It was Arbor Day in May.

What baffles me still—though I know the ending?
Willowy girl in batiste blouse and pencil skirt,
coronet of auburn braids that might have toppled
another standing less gracefully erect than you;
missing but hinted, are freckles which, in person,
sprinkled your face like peppergrass seeds after frost.

How does a poem begin? For needing to hear your voice
(and want of a yet to be invented sound camera) and
my separation from that which is inseparable from you:
THE LAUREL SONG BOOK by M. Teresa Armitage,
1914?
Budding minds flowered from it and your pitch pipe:
Words to Andante Cantabile, music by Verdi and Bach.
We sang our insides out for Stephen Foster and "Nancy
Lee"
excelled ourselves with "Darkey" before Race became
a six-letter word and we knew the melody was
Humoreske.

After fifty years disuse I gave the book to Nina
who shares her gifts, enriching worn minds of many

who remember when "Love's Old Sweet Song" was
young.

Looking farther into the photo it comes to mind
you might be nearing ninety now, but little older than
the children here, failure—and worse—ahead:
For lack of discipline an unrenewed contract.
The big boys were sorry for their clumsy pranks.
Did anyone tell you this in that kinder climate
for consumptives where you died so far from us?

Hear now our Miss Holley ending each day's turmoil,
sending us off to home chores, not a child of us to
dream
a future when her practice, which should be told/retold,
would come to be a gnawing bone for Church and
State.
Preceding your sung-prayer we faltered two verses:
"America"
and then you soloed the haunting English roundelay.
We closed
our eyes,
sensing it was too beautiful to endure,
too gentle in the harshness of that time:
"Goodnight to you all, and sweet be your sleep,
May angels around you their silent watch keep.
Goodnight   Goodnight   Goodnight . . ."

Goodnight, dear Margaret, forever nineteen:
I hear you   I hear you   I hear you . . .

Postscript

My beloved used to say,
"Only when we give away
what we really want to keep—
and know the times to sow or reap—
do we receive the best reward."

A poem for Margaret was overdue,
and what he said is true. Is true!

The Moldau at Our Door

(for my father, John W. Kritz, 1870–1947)

In the spring of my years
whippoorwills hushed the diurnal birds
but no one told me about night people and day people.
The wild horses of winter heaved our walls
and Loki came to the bedside
where I lay awaiting opossum and owls.

That summer night held a new dimension
from wind or pond or tree.
Then sounds became footsteps
and a moaning in the room below.
Breath crackled in my parchment throat
so sure I was it must be the peddler come at dusk,
dressed like death in flapping cape,
a kind of trunk strapped to his back.
We had tittered at his trembling
till Father froze us with a look, and said to him,
"We've a cot in the summer shanty, if you care to stay.
There'll be no moon till morning."
He almost cried, I saw—
and Father sent us for blanket and supper plate.
From our tent of twilight we children
had spied on him inside the shed, pacing,
food untouched, saw him pound his head
like a hawk we captured once.
Now, in my parents' bed were whisperings,
a frightened, "I hear him!
Someone's in the house and moving 'round."
"Bolt the bedroom door," Father said,
"when I go down."
He speared the monster night with a struck match,
lit the lamp, and silenced her alarm.

He put his trousers on and went,
a dark and terrible and a gentle man.

Up the stairwell came his voice:
"We need you, Kristine. Hurry!"

I knelt beside the chamber on the floor,
too sick for prayers.
Through the register I heard my father say,
"I'll have a neighbor go, if you're afraid."
I dared to peer into the room below:
the stranger sat, bare and hairy to the waist;
his half-crooked arm, swollen twice its size,
lay like cow's liver on our table.
Mother was at wringing out a towel, saying,
"You get the doctor, John."

He stayed with us awhile,
conjured magic from that trunk
with linen, tapestries and lace.
"The Wandering Jew" he called himself,
this countryman of Father's.
Evening they talked the Moldau to our farm.
When they sang,
we heard the forest with our eyes,
and stars rolled up toward heaven
like lava from Wisconsin's valley.
The stream purled out in cashmere scarves
and whippoorwills went hoarse.

He left us when the season changed to fall—
in me a hint of all the autumns yet to be;
and returns, an Indian summer wraith,
half a century tall
on days when symphonies are televised

for twenty millions to learn from Bernstein
what rivers say—the Mississippi, Danube, Styx—
I who never heard an orchestra
communed with Smetana
before his music met ears which hear him as no other;
the roar and murmurings, the anthem,
made a tapestry forever summer, pain, compassion,
and the Moldau running past our door.

A Summer Day that Changed the World

All the way down the valley the house where Kristin
is going to visit can be seen. Over hills
from home she knows it well—but last night in her
dream
it changed to a quarry where skeletons were found.

The mare, Beauty, sun-bleached, often sun-blind and
heavesy
is dependable and their only riding horse.
Balloon-wide to sit astride her little girl legs
stick out like seal flippers, are wobbly afterward.
It is better than walking three miles to the house
built onto the hill. She thinks about its strangeness:
Incense, on the floors creamy bears with no insides,
birds that talk back, showy flowers she never knew,
wall-hangings to be put out of her country mind.
Windows high for her seeing out are hung with boughs
—They say its name, Taliesen, means Shining Brow.
She does not like the place, but neither do Martha
and John who vacation here a month each summer.
The children want to go home. She will not tattle,
or tell them what grown-ups say about their mother.
It is not that they are different, only rich,
so she wears her nearly best clothes. When told
she should not visit there because of "Goings-on"
her father asked, "Are not the children innocent?"
They seldom had company, and Kristin knew why
she had been invited: When her father was young
he worked for maiden aunts who ran Hillside Home
School.
Autumns, winters, springs he drove double-span Morgans
back/forth to town for students farmed from city homes.
The school is closed and scary now. It is summer.

Saturday, our Lady's Assumption in August,
Church again tomorrow. Oxeye daisies suggest
picking for the altar, gophers run a rickrack
across dusty roads. Their pretty valley dozes
that near-noon hour. Beside the buildings grain is
 stacked
ready for threshing, binders put away in sheds.
Full of happy news and hurry-up she urges
Beauty on with a slap, remembering too late
the collar sore. But joy sustains: She is to ask
the children to her place for watching the thresher
 work.
Despite coaxing Get-aps! the mare stops, head lifted,
nosing air.

Smoke out front? No more than from a stove
at first but soon the whole hill wears a ruffled cap
of smoke. A scream! Others—men voices—children
 cries—
sounds running together like wildness of night winds.
She slides to the ground and crawls toward Willow
 Walk,
then climbs between the triple trunks of a gnarled one
where once she and Martha had played house with their
 dolls.
Smoke coming nearer now—hoarsened voices—Quiet!
Is this still dreaming—bones in the quarry turned black?
Kristin looks at her trembling hands, begins to cry,
prays: "Hail Mary, full of grace! The Lord is with
 thee . . ."
over and over again: "The Lord is with me."
It is bad to be nearly nine and so afraid,
fire on the hill, screaming less, the children quiet—
She did not come for this Thing—whatever it is—
an unknown that is sensed all around the willows,

troubling and secret as reasons the house is strange.
"The Lord is with me . . . The Lord is with me . . . The
Lord

They have found Beauty. She hears them calling,
"Kristin!
Kristeene!" The tree holds her up but no answer comes,
father-arms lifting her from darkness she fights, breath-
taste
like fresh blood as from running too fast. No more tears.

They climb the stone stairs to tell people she is safe,
cross the court past covered shapes like statues in Lent
fallen over. One that is half under towels,
hair burned and lashes from eyes that beg: Stay with me!
Please don't go! The lips move to form her name:
"Kristin—"
She is mute yet sees on the blackboard of her mind
the lie: THAT IS NOT MARTHA—even as she knows
the September-sapphires ring on the swollen hand.
She moves ahead of her father, drawing him on,
aware of other men in sooty, bloodied clothes,
their faces sweat-striped masks barely recognizable.

Mother is having a spell. Neighbors rub her wrists,
wipe her face. Kristin can smell the digitalis,
sweat from hot arms around them, and stranger's breath.
Not for such attention of to lessen their fears
has she come so far to what is best learned alone—
though foreshadowed when crossing the River in flood,
seeing whirlpools and undertow that take lives,
wild reflections of sky. At such times her inside-
voices clearly repeated AVES she could not
for heartbeats flipflapping like trout out of water.

More people come to look, to judge. Kristin listens:
"The gardener spoke before he died. It was that black
devil Julian." No! Kristin thinks, Not the new cook.
Julian makes better desserts than anyone else!
But who would care? "This was bound to happen!" they
say,
and "The wages of sin!" and then "The will of God!"
are like two strings for their beady words. "Be watchful
children," they warn, "Don't go near the walls or
ledges."
Don't and Do: "Don't get dirty! Do stay in plain view!"
So they play Racetrack, and Trains on the concrete strips
that lead into the cold furnace—all but Kristin
who sits cross-legged to keep her knees from shaking,
and watches a spot under the rubble where smoke
rises as if a teakettle were boiling there.
This day has erased the dream she tries to recall—
but afterwards remembered when John is not found.
Anxious to leave with her father for the depot
they meet a train that brings two men sharing sorrow;
One whose love-house it was. One whose children they
were.
Up those steps again in deep shadows of late dusk,
changed as summer and the valley, changed as Kristin
leaving the last sheltered season of innocence.
(O generations!—Whatever it is we are—
never the same after some ruined hill is climbed
and we meet face to face the Thing that makes it
Was.)

Reality goes into a created well,
a darkness for those unfamiliar names of sins,
hatchet truth in the hands of a servant gone *berserk*.
She does relive that longest night after the fire

when a posse tramped the bypaths, their howling
hounds
blood-calling WHOO AWHOO AWHOOO, along
the creek
and into a stone quarry that opens the caves.
Sickish again hearing them, all the HAIL MARYS
stick between the pages of her tongue and palate
until sleepiness crowds her like the mare against
a barn stall when not in the mood to be ridden.
Then there is Julian, liver-color and crouched
on all fours in that furnace, and his teeth are like
unbaked ladyfingers. Kristin wakes dry retching,
afraid to move in the big bed upstairs alone,
till she hears whippoorwills and knows she has dreamed.
Into the well goes singed bearskin rugs, gutted rooms
with shapes beneath blankets and smells best forgotten,
parts to be hidden away—some for years and years.
But when nocturnal creatures converse in the woods
and she is thoughtful, snatches return unbidden:
One man watching with folded arms while another
weeps over rubble, raking with blackened fingers
in trickling smoke for bones eleven summers young—
his son—and the scarlet shame burning her back
forever turned away from eyes that begged—
eyes bluer fire than birthstone sapphire.

NOTE: This is an eyewitness account of the fire on August 15, 1914, at the Wyoming Valley home of Frank Lloyd Wright. Eight persons died, five adults and three children.

Early Rock—Christmas 1916

Kristin was satiated with opera:
Feodor Chaliapin, Ernestine Schumann-Heink,
John McCormack and his Christmas carols.
These singers try too hard, she thought,
as the thick, black disks spun round and round.
The EDISON's magic was gone. When BOHEMIAN
GIRL
arias filled their parlor she no longer heard.
Her needs were again for gentle sounds of nature:
rustles in trees before moonrise and after sunrise
wind-minors under the eaves, other voices in between.
Besides that, Kristin had been to Chautaqua.
Fresh currents flowed from somewhere out there:
The spidery music from China, Hawaiian swirls,
uneasy throbbings from the Dark Continent.
Since Chautauqua she was filled with zeal
to go there and save the heathen.

This particular day was for providing against winter.
Last evening brother Leo had carried buckets of water
to the cast iron feed kettle, then Father built a fire
underneath it, inside its wall of stones.
Kristin lay abed listening to grunts and squeals,
then to high wails dwindling as life flowed away
into a clean pan. Blood sausage was an unfavored food.

Now she could go outside and watch as the two hogs
were lowered with pulley and rope, one by one,
into the scalding bath, then the scraping with knives
until their skins were whiter than hers. Stakes,
sharp at both ends, forced under hind leg tendons
were for hoisting again to make gutting easier.
Kristin waited patiently. She had a plan.
When livers, sweetbreads and hearts were in a washtub

to be taken to the pump for cleansing and cooling
she touched her father's chin: "May I have the
bladders?"
"Whatever for?" he asked, then, "I suppose so. But
mind
you be careful handling them?" She understood: hands
away
from one's face. Afterwards wash with hot water and
soap.

The process was painstaking. She wondered, as each
rinse
was expelled, how the bladders pulsed like living hearts
until with the vinegar and salt solution this stopped.
She used straws saved from sasparilla treats
with which to inflate them before inserting handles
of peeled hickory sticks. Set aside in a jar
were a dozen little round creek pebbles—*all* to hide
in an attic for drying. It was October.

Well before Christmas everything was ready.
They would do their own concert for the school
program:
TURKEY IN THE STRAW, DO LORD, I SAW
THREE SHIPS,
YANKEE DOODLE, JESUS IS A ROCK IN A
WEARY LAND—
Leo on harmonica, she with her homemade maracas.
Are you listening, child of today?
They brought down the house.

Where the Bittersweet Grew

Homing from lessons, Kristin has trouble
traversing a ridge-field where stubble
of sorghum cane and timothy hay
challenge her footing this chilly day.

(It is well that Newton's steers are gone
—the pasture creek was her Rubicon—
often afraid and glad for the haul
that took them to market in early fall.)

Beside the field is a rocky retreat
all bloodied red with bittersweet.
Kristin knows she is not to take
even a sprig of this mythic heartache.

Uneasy, she figures that cowards run
lest darkness outdistance the setting sun,
recalls how Father, at seeding time,
crossed himself when he told the crime:

"A banished husband, heavy with hate
returned to murder and violate;
then out of madness or oversight
he left their child alone that night

"And no one there to tend his wants,
nor any concerned with the foreign Brandts.*
—The child with his mother and grandmother dead!"
(Kristin thinks that she would have fled!)

*Mary Murphy, 1848–1903 (grandmother), Mary Murphy Brandt, 1875–1903 (wife & mother)

Evenings later the four-year-old
was found unconscious from hunger and cold.
Then James Lloyd Jones took Martin to rear
who ten years after would disappear.

"The boy was lacking in gratitude!"
they said in stern solicitude.
Of the Valley secrets never a sign,
while gossip rolled on tongues like wine:

"Son of a killer who hanged himself
with strips attached to a prison shelf.
'Or maybe the women had sin to conceal?
They had been seen with Rose O'Neill!' "

Kristin, listening did not suspect
that a day would come to recollect,
to write about what Martin faced—
a trauma never fully erased . . .

> O better to tell of the marble stone
> with a lamb reclining as if to atone
> his father's guilt: Whatever the case
> how Martin came back to mark the place
>
> In St. Luke's ground the Marys lie
> mute to the questioning passerby;
> forgotten the terror and tragedy
> that night in nineteen-hundred-and-three.

Here in this Valley that Martin knew,
over hillside rocks where bittersweet grew,
Kristin has heard such wind-borne cries
as saddens her more than terrifies.

Farmer's Wife

The years like black oxen
Cattle filing from barn to pasture
The young woman, migraine inured to kaleidoscopic
    sparks,
lingered in the open driveway's draft.
Milking smells behind her, and welcome breeze
rumoring June primroses and cured hay,
the real light beyond the barn shadows
fell like a whip to her eyes.
Sound became illusory
as the morning sickness began again.
She talked to herself, forcing coherency:
How'll I get through this day!
—a fifth anniversary picnic   schemers
their Old World jokes that stale—
I'm twenty-three   Another life begins in me
a child shouldn't be made of snake blood
loveless recoil   How many more?
Like winter sparrows her future massed:
Each year a child. (Some would die.)
The carried water pail running out of sight,
washboard and farmer clothes,
meals an endless belt,
coarsening acceptance of slaughter, animal needs.
—The stallion screaming kicked his corral.

Breakfast. Four to dress for church.
Then the long drive to the Grotto Spa,
that raised in her a gale for flight—
no one of them forgiven her misery, except the babies.

Tying on bibs, she studied the complacent ones
who mapped her life as if it were crop land:
doting mother-in-law spooning salads, beans;
the grandfathers carving meat and melon.

A shadow hunts with the wolf: She felt her husband's
    eyes
devouring her till his other hunger prevailed.
Tears fell on the infant she changed; softly she said,
You'll be better off   darlings   all of you
They will think I fell   but I will run and not look
Grass is for the feet of the runner   Run

She accepted the full plate. Nausea   RUN

A flight behind the Grotto were cliffs and the river.
She slipped away to a place abandoned at noontime
and shut the picnic area from view.
Faster over stony path without ceremony of torchbearer
she circled shadowing Stations of the Cross,
tripped and fell at the tenth.

Someone was turning her gently over. . . .
She looked to the arcade for a wing flicker, any sign
not of her conscience, flint or fire.
In tidal wave a terrible fish moved its tail.
She was herself the catch—a sturgeon, muscles torn—
lifted struggling from dark water on the spear of life.
When she got to her feet the embryo,
tinting the stones, glistened like fresh roe,
her eyes with the salt of reprieve.

The Rose Jar

—for my parents

1

They lie now in the vacant embrace
of seasons vast as earth horizons
where passion and love endured
till eye-dials became agates
and the hands of yesterdays
fell from memory and faded.

In this rose jar are nearly half a century's
fragments. It is a petaled anthology
of bridal bouquets and boutonnieres,
anniversary and baptismal forget-me-nots,
orchids of prom and casket spray . . .

2

I hold glued together shards,
its cover like a mended eggshell:
    The ever-listening little girl
    whose gather is going to an auction
    hears her mother say, "Kate had two ham pots.
    Our big kettle has sprung another leak."
    Bending to kiss us, he promises to buy one.
    All afternoon I wait his return.
    He has bought three sheep and a bull calf
    and something rolled up in a grain bag.
    In the house he unwraps a foot high rose jar.
    I see on his inner lighted face a look
    (like that cameras were to record in mine)
    The draining away to dismay. She is angry.
    He must explain again how his bid on the pot
    was lost. Done, he adds, "But I only paid

sixty cents for a remembrance of Kate."
—Ancient poetry about hyacinths and bread
still unknown, I knew whose child I was—
She smashed the cover on the durable jar.
Holding only its knob, her contrition began.

3

Dusk and wind rising against glories of afterglow:
Beyond vistas of cowled hills and Interstate road
which was the wilderness where this State commenced,
any-and-every place barometric angers rise and fall,
faiths weaken, love falters. Men and women, now
more than then, spent of spirit go down
in mindless defeat to incipient surfeit
as northern earth succumbs to November,
while others triumph in elsewhere climates
as saffron, canna, azaleas and roses blaze.

Oh! Here in that time at this homesite
youth was a fleeting phantom, kin to weather,
and love and dreams were boy and girl together.
But in this time at that homesite the mislaid
plans for remakes of outmoded romance scatter
like old scenarios over a ghostly set.
Only regret is at large to tremble
at unnatural wind sirens warning
up the distances of years.

4

I am consoled and possessed
by an R S Prussia rose jar
and the memories it holds.

Such a Child's Waiting

(For Howard Edward Meudt, 1926–1936)

Believing children once were mine—
a benison
that is the reversible cloak of life.

Imperishable one!
the fabric of you is everglaze
though inclemency darkened your bright plaid.

Decembers number twenty-two
since REA retired lamp and lantern oil—
and diminished the list for Relief.

Solemnly
waiting to run his errands
my son rubbed beeswax over the sled-runners.
"Kathy wants a new one," he said,
but she should wish for overshoes—
We will have our baby soon?"
Pungency struck like sadiron kissing wax.
I nodded dumbly
in that open-season for lists
when children strained hope-combs
for their happiness-honey.

The ironing board has run the gamut
from sackcloth to silicon
since the day I bent above it writing:
raisins and sago, sugar, cinnamon
and sausage for a special treat.
When he returned I took the groceries
and held an open hand for change.
Beneath his cerebellic eyes

the winter peaches ripened;
his voice was a willow-whistle:
"I plan to earn the money spent—
I have to show the things I bought?"
(No tardy pardons for this lash between my teeth!)
Hearing the verdict he fetched them in:
a ten-cent paring knife,
("I—me and Dick," he said, "We broke your other
    one")
a string of Christmas lights—
green and gold and red and and blue.

I turned away that dusk.

The child went in and laid his Magian-gifts
upon the cluttered table-top,
and carried in the wood
and did some other chores.
The evening meal was done.

My son stood close to whisper:
"After school—I could take them back tomorrow."
Cooling whimsy blew a smile for him.
(The strength it took to face that breeze again!)
"We will keep them, dear," I said.

The boy we could not keep.
He never saw the little pine, knife-pared to symmetry,
alight in green and gold and red and blue.

Now is the redundant season
when the symbol
subject to cold appraisal
shows garish . . . I listened:
"The newer trims are toward artistic unity."

"A tree should complement one's color scheme."
"You have a burned-out bulb-set there."
Silently
the tree said, Joy and Sorrow, Affection and Faith.
The opalescent angels spoke,
and every green and gold and red and blue
told of other Christmases ago.

"Not unity," I mused, "But continuity."

Ah, love, this tree for shelter!
Across my shoulders is the tartan of remembrance,
and such a child's waiting warms me.

Rex—A Dog to Be Remembered

He was white with touches of chestnut,
mostly collie, some part shepherd, the only dog
we ever bought—and this despite debts,
Depressions's aftermath and two years drought.
The circumstance was odd: A person, seedy
as his truck, drove in one day selling pups.
That these might be stolen did not occur to us,
so inward-occupied we were—having lost a boy.

The little sisters wanted all (or any) of the puppies.
For the eldest (and now the only son) there came
an instant, automatic love for this older one.
Reluctantly their father paid the spot cash,
perceiving in me a rising anger had he not.
Richard, eleven then and having read Terhune,
thought to call him "Rex." We acquiesed and none
could guess how well the name would fit,
or that later we might attribute to him royal blood
—such was his demeanor and sense of duty.
A trustier baby-sitter never served, shadowing them
to kill a snake or rodents. He could also entertain.

Rex had a built-in clock that told him when to fetch
the milk cows from the pasture, when to take them
back;
how to head-off feeder pigs, and timing his nip
and then avoid the horses' hooves at round-up.
Ordinary folk, we took this good servant as our due,
his wages always lean, as growing children / hungry
men
make scarce the table scraps. A reproachful look
often sent me foraging. I never had such thanks
for homemade bread from any of my kin.

Neighbor and stranger alike recognized a presence
to be reckoned with—except in times of storm:
An outside, working dog he heard the far-off
thunder first, whimpered his concern and fright.
We'd check the radio, and soon (at Richard's entreaty)
I was mellowed to let Rex in the kitchen where he crept
beneath the table, his muzzle on any foot around.
When lightning crackled so close we smelled its
    elements
he was rendered incontinent. We puzzled then
if some ancient catastrophe might have hidden in him
unwelcome genes, for afterward he was meek with
    shame—
yet all the wisdom of dogs flickered in his hazel eyes.

The wind that April Sunday morning was savage
even for this Uplands. I was dressing a toddler for Mass
when Richard, washing in an anteroom, saw smoke:
The great overland barn, old and heaving in the storm,
friction caused wires to break and dangle in a hayloft.
"The cattle! The cattle! And the horses!" the menfolk
    shouted,
while I ran out and called "Rex!" Lightning streaks of
    fire,
wind-driven, flashed from between the barn's loose
    boards.
Matt, a hired man, had thrown the switch to release
cows from stanchions, nonetheless frightened beasts
do freeze and will not leave a burning building.
Briefly Rex hesitated, for that instant fear
overpowering duty, then barking, snarling, teeth bared,
vicious in his own dread of the unknowable, he went in
and drove them out. Refusing to be led, the horses too
    obeyed.
The calves in pens he could not save although he tried,
while fire and smoke singed him brown and almost
    blind.

On blistered footpads he found me in the gathering
crowd.
Stroking him I saw his eyes were shut, and cried, "He's
blind!
Rex is blind!" Then Richard, who had been searching,
came
and would not have it so. Arms around his dog, buried
face
in burnt fur the kneeling boy cried softly in that furious
place.
Hearing his muffled prayer I added mine, "He isn't
blind?
Rex can't be that kind of dog? Dear Jesus, Please!"

A week or more we kept him bedded near the Monarch
range,
limbs salved and wrapt in worn-out bedsheets torn in
strips.
The children bathed his eyes in antiseptic and saline
waters
while I was busy with meals for neighbors who came to
help
with cleanup and building shelters for the livestock.
Rex seemed to understand his hero-role. Walking past
into the dining room, some would pause to offer praise.
I thought and said, "If it's possible for dogs to envy cats
it must be now. Rex has a need to purr."
Though not blind,
he was never the same, had lost a perspicacity, caution
about
his daily chores: once came too close the tractor's
wheels.
Afterwards he went on three legs only and never raced
with autumn's blown leaves or phantom rabbits again.

His counted time with us was seven years of days:
hardship days, exuberance days going by like snails

or kited seeds. His last November Richard went to
        W.W. II.

We stood against a fence fiery-eyed with bittersweet,
a fearful mother   the whimpering dog.

Requiem for Communication Lines and Power Poles

On the blade's edge of Old Military Ridge
we drove at summer's end, I fighting estrangement,
afraid to ask of self: *Have I been away that long?*
At the wheel a daughter spoke, "It's good to see
so far without ugly poles wherever one looks."
Broken sod in strips showed burial site of wires.
"It's a dark day that robs the swallows," I said.

(Beloved, I will miss our music staffs along skies
a dozen years *Sunset and evening* star-scanned.
How do I know you went West? Tennyson? Whitman?)

North is the Valley where some stone
must remember a young man, gaunt as the Fifth
Horseman from grimmest race: "Had we a telephone
our sister Frances might have been saved."

If whippoorwills hand down legends, do they tell
in the ravaged hickory near the roothouse door
of another sister moaning nights over days
in agony of breech-birthing a twin, one fetus
undetected death in the womb?

Summer 1910 communication lines strung a splendor
between our dark hills. In the kitchen
Mother cranking our phone, lifted a black trumpet
from its wishbone cradle, said, "Viele grusse, Frieda!"
Then again: "Bridgit? Top of the evenin' to you!"
Too late for saying *Glaedeligs* or other
Danish phrases none ever greeted her!

(And you who knew each marrow-bedded scar—
old circles break! I raise the memory trumpet
for your gentle philosophizing: "Mankind's powers
of adjustment are seemingly limitless.")

Still the question: What will the swallows do?
Return to what it was before there were barns
and irresistable wires? Or must they go
as the passenger pigeon with the whooping crane?

When pieces of silver
become a price with stigma
question the traders well.

Only God sells Himself eternally.

The Round River Canticle

One of the marvels of early Wisconsin was the Round River, a river that flowed into itself, and thus sped around and around in a never ending circuit. Paul Bunyan discovered it, and the Bunyan saga tells how he floated many a log on its restless waters.

—Aldo Leopold

I

This canticle is of love,
simple and shimmering as a view of river;
turbulent and mysterious with undertow.
It is sonorous and full, a song of many rivers
running to seas that wash forever
in the azure tide where all love goes.

It is muted and soft,
the cadence of his heart
whose ebb and flow was the river around
my life.

II

Auctioned to an unfriendly world
I traveled neither forth and back nor up.
It was October over hills
where the wild grape went ungathered,
and late jackdaws mocked me—
a straw woman wanting a river.

You were found in springtime,
a current strong and swift with season,
shadowed in onyx and ambers
oh you were inaccessible and far.

Even then I glimpsed the gelding winter
reflected in separating waters.
How avidly it waited to trample
where the owls hooted I would not see,
nor would I believe the crying loons.
I thought to go around winter
to your sunny banks.

I went with tunes of sandpipers and widgeons,
whistled with snipe across the meadows,
and visited with chattering teal
as dusk came up from the marshes.

III

On a cameo beach I wakened
to the leap of sunbeams combing your riffles,
and was swept into wonder.
You were dawn's ethereal stillness
in the month of first Masses
but I heard the roaring cataclysm
of transubstantiation
as wheat in the chaff of me came to life.

In my reborn eyes you were as silver nitrate
insuring purity of vision.
But in no chapter and verse is the miracle told
of how I crossed your waters
to waken and find you
in every moment and fragment
of experience.

IV

Thereafter I was lintel-lashed
on a round river island

where hydrology was studied
and never understood.
I knew expanses of translunar moods,
your freshets and backwaters, bars and small
whirlpools. I knew your warmth
and plummeted your floorless deeps.

To mire me in doubts
rare disquietudes overflowed you
on whose silt the island biota flourished.

I became a prototype of paradox and parables:
going nowhere, all things came to me;
merely *being*, I fed the mainstream of you
who spoke to multitudes.

Then summer with her triple-tongued sun
of duty, ambition and old loyalties
came to lap you.

V

Drouth was the summer day
you were lost somewhere in shifting sandbars,
and I waited on the bedlam banks
while darkness was riveted over with stars.

All night I was there
till a golden discus was flung
skimming crystal that broke in concentric circles,
like a monstrance lifted to your silver crest.

In the southeast potted clouds boiled
over this raging sunfire,
and fear crackled through copper grass
to my dry cell eyes.

Who was it turned the wind that day
to blow clean from some Andean peak
to fill the rain-gathering clouds and quicken you?
I saw the live clouds, flowered
into racemes and panicles of hyacinth and lilac,
refined in you.

VI

Other seasons followed, when nightly I crept bedside
for reassurance that your lifestream flowed.

The time for planting being long fled,
our honey locusts were young ladies
who clicked their castanets and spread sequined skirts,
and curtsying, each was like a school of shining
minnows.

There were autumn games to enjoy:
the pole vaulting beavers, and fullback squirrel
clutching butternut and running for touchdown.

I was terrorized
by testudines of cyanotic turtles*
and loons that spread the late obituaries
in plicated papyrus.

The arts were revaluated:
sculpture, in the philosophic silence of bone;
the euphonies of shells, of legs in friction,
of eliding wings, and labials of wind;
the calligraphy of burl and leaf;
the masterpieces of sunrise, and evening sky.

*(The reference is to the fingernails and skin of persons who suffer from severe coronary insufficiency.)

VII

It was autumn again—
the promise in your springtime glance fulfilled,
and I did not know.
The windsongs were scored to themes of Where or
When,
and I did not hear.
The osiers leaned to the mirror of you
and flushed the faces of days.

Harvest is at hand—
the vintage of grape, and largess of fruit and kernel
garnered from October hills—
and nature's lares and penates
wear a patina of your dear omnipresence.

There was this little time
to function in the hydrology of faith:
in anointments and unitings,
bread dispensed, and the poured ablutions—
reenactments of Genesareth and Jordan.

If I noted saplings where your backwaters were
I would not see the freshets too were gone,
nor admit the slow declension of your body
a calling back to ocean and prebirth.

VIII

Wild-eyed and toothless, winter stormed its last,
his nightmare mane trailing over the tension of days.
It was a winter of elements gone mad
and owl music in the willows.

Once more, far down the hemispheres
the equinoctial princes stirred,
and waking, murmured April.

I do not care how long
God spent creating earth.
I saw you stilled.

Darling,
what did He do to the world
when you died?

IX

Give me one sign
lest metrical hills
weary of my endless scansion.

Oh turn this way,
turn this way your luminist smile
over these water-color and tracings of days.

Come to me.
Find me in the jade-veined country
where your yesterdays flowed.

Where locks are levels of mist,
under bridges of shadow,
enter Love's infinite ocean.

Farm Woman

Is it time to ask of going away? Another year
is into summer, one which divided by four
comes out even to make a Leap Year. A Leap Year?
When I was young it gave a girl
license to signal the boy of her choice.
The solicitory overture was not yet an ERA.

The barns are gone now. Livestock do not graze.
Horses are eunuchs and mares like odalisques.
The herdsire is milked. Cows and hens, de-animalized,
become factories, their life cycles measured in pounds
of protein/fat, quotas of eggs.

All last summer while we sweltered,
flowers in dead grasses pleaded with sky.
Pollens routed the woolly molds.
That lush siren September fooled no one:
As the particle seen of a flying thing
with every color fell the shadow promising winter.

Is it time to ask of going away?
Seventy-nine years waver like echoing voices.
I brought children into this world: They were good
sons,
dying young. I bore daughters, more distant.

These Uplands have served my spirit well:
Studied for revelation, the silences probed
for signs from those who bequeathed this loneliness.
I hoped for faith and loved the hope.
Now there is left the integrity of these hills,
trust and the questions: Is it time to ask
directions for going away?

Return to Place of Hawks

We came to your present place, concrete
under sod and marble bench, crossed the road
and nature plot to the stone house deep in oaks.

Your mother welcomed us, pretty pink as wild rose.
Reminiscence held in shadows against stairwell
and ceiling. We spoke of guests along those years:
Early Mr. Wright had come—"Derleth, you've built
yourself a barn," he said, and heard, "Why not, Frank?
A bull will be living in it."

                                        But we know
you had a man's most gentle ways—how the big hands
could touch a friend, on typewriter keys loosen music
to turn words dimensional as these pine knotted walls,
where bone weary, undefeated you sensed your *time.*

Then in the kitchen for tea your mother waited
as we drank silence of her house peopled with books
and a permanence of you. We saw over phlox and fern
the cemetery, through open windows caught the high
"Come here! Come here!" of a *tyrannus* kingbird
waiting too for the whine of death to make him whole.

North Star

(on the 104th Anniversary of Mother's birth,
after reading "A REPORT FROM THE EMPTY
GRAVE" by Daniel Berrigan, S.J.)

This first day of spring, imagination lit, I try to find
that roof-thatcher's cottage in the fishing city of Vejle.
Mother, I wish we might visit this entire ice-melting
day,
I mean VISIT, after preliminary greetings are spent,
say to you that I have expiated insensitivity
to your homesickness, how carried like an undergarment
rash
the trivia of my untouchableness most of those years.
I have made amends less with printed words than
personal change,
in relationships being accessible and more patient.

If you are unchanged you will want to know reasons I
have come,
why the discarded hairshirt, engage me in hypotheses?
Priest-poet Daniel Berrigan has written of menial tasks
and solace given in terminal cancer wards, "Where I can
do more for my dying country, for my church, for my
order."
Remember the notebooks your child filled with
philosopher's quotes?
"In Paris alone where no one cared for me, and where
my soul
fell back on itself without finding there either God or
faith
but only pride of anticipated glory, I understood
I had been preaching Pere Lacordaire instead of Christ-
crucified."

You observe that I have come full circle back to
Lacordaire?
Yes. I believe others moralize, are neither deaf nor blind,
though tragically mute in disillusion and cancerous
doubts
over the dissolution of the Great American Dream,
the Christian dream, United Nations, dreams ad
infinitum.
This favored country was never the Eden of Genesis
nor is it now a terminal case though it may need criers
as mother countries suffered Savonarolas and Luthers
rolling their carts, wakening us to bring out the
casualties.
Which does not mean we disclaim humor in irrational
times
when Gore Vidal suggests Fonda for first distaff
President.
I have digressed to make for twenty-five years an ice-
breaker:
Your last birthday spent with us, we took you home to
sleep away.
What kind of goodbye was that! Useless to dwell on
this each night
undressing beside your carved oak bed and drawing over
me
the brown/gold coverlet pieced and quilted in North
Star design.
Flashing needles, tales of cutter-captain brothers are
recalled
but never a voicetone unless somehow the dead speak
through us.
(We are self-consciously more precise, or literal-minded,
than in William's day when Hamlet, finished conversing
with ghost
of his father soliloquizes: "That undiscovered country
from whose bourne no traveler returns!") Ah yes!
ramblings, as is

the want with spectral visits when one must ask and
answer, both.
The unanswered questions! Did you assimilate the equal
parts
Jesus Christ, Martin Luther, John Calvin in
grandmother's milk?
Oh how well I would listen now while you told of
Danish ways,
the dreaded leechings and mud packs baked on boils
before a fire—
terrors to damage a young heart; of all such midwifery.
You would tell of sailing alone for America, this date
your eighteenth natal day, looking back till Thumbelina-
sized
the harbor Mermaid created from Hans Andersen genius
and Thorvaldsen bronze; of first glimpsing Bartholdi's
masterwork,
that Goddess of Liberty born of France's faith in the
ideal,
chiseled below with Lazarus' concern for our growing
pains.
Aboard ship was the new correspondent homing from
China
who must have anticipated debarkment as Orpheus
looked his last on Eurydice (judging from pictures he
made.)
I would share excitement passing Bedloe to Ellis Island,
buildings three months new, multi-windowed, roof
towers of blue slate.

That April year blows in my mind like flint sand:
Winter ravaged
opportunity-land reviewed from Union Pacific train,
coming to the maelstrom of Chicago's Columbian Fair.
Mid-November I would go shopping with you for
family gifts

marveling at your knowledge of adopted language and
mores
help you select for your parents the velvet photo album
on silver mounting, bound with rich brass bands
hammered to likeness
of Columbus. Would either of us be able to believe
that today I could fetch from its place of honor this
album
your mother filled with pictures become like leaves of
yesteryears?
Turning its pages you might name who they were I
never knew,
while they step forward breathing again in the only
sunlight
and air we earthlings know. If necessary I will explain
how your sister Anna's son, dear cousin Johs., ever
thoughtful
sent it here to honor your one-hundredth anniversary.

When these hours are over I will be like Emily, bereft
for OUR TOWN that was, for the Valley where,
March nineteen-o-six,
my presence within your body was confirmed.
Plain-spoken now,
you safe from fears and panic of reliving a first ordeal,
I strip away pretenses to wonder if your intolerance
to pain sparked my indifference to physical discomfort?
Or are these Father's genes? And do you commune with
him out there,
merry with his brothers? Father a Justice Holmes look-
alike—
(So his descendants say.) Are you young as I recall you
young?
Or diminished as when you waited seven years alone?

Which brings us to Acts of Contrition too glibly recited,

BALTIMORE CATECHISM lessons too easily
memorized
not to please God or you but for the gentle pastor I
loved
the only one a child dared to ask about Bible vengeance.
A day during persecution of German Americans
I came upon him weeping, cradled his head in my girl-
arms
(even as the blue velvet album, Love's prefiguration.)

A third quarter moon understates this vernal equinox
as we go now to celebrate—your namesake, her children
and I—at the restaurant designed by neighbor Frank
Lloyd Wright
(aloof towards us but who with Father never outgrew
friendship.)
Does disembodied spirit gain in forbearance, compassion
in ration with time-lapse, to accept a granddaughter who
plies
the most ancient profession? I need to know for when
we meet
in your "bourne" no longer confront me as a daughter
made helpless
by obedient hypocrisy but as that later woman
grown strong to recognize the mockery of arranged
wedlock,
given courage to realize some laws of earth well lost for
love.

A few evening stars are signalling this reverie must cease.
Father Berrigan, closing out his Empty Grave Report
says
of epiphany: "At least one of those stars stood firm: The
North Star
gave point to action above, direction to action below."

These of his words were the starting place for mine.
Typically
I come to them at the end. Thanks to you I was better
versed
than most in Holy and Polaris lore. Oh that the beacon
of the former guide me still as steadily as the later
in that bleeding void beyond! I recall you tensing my
mind
between the hell of North Sea fury and Heaven's
infinity,
saying, "My brothers were not lost. There was always
the North Star!"

On the calendar of movable feasts this early Eastertide
a final constant: The season's first whippoorwill pair are
back.
In blackness of pre-dawn I heard them far away in the
hills,
as one by one the stars blinked out, chanting their own
TENEBRAE.

Part IV

Over My Shoulder (And Some Shadows)

"How often I question and doubt whether that is really Me."
—Walt Whitman

There were, first of all, the non-writers, my parents. Mother cherished and kept for me the fine, leatherbound volumes of Byron, Tennyson, Moore, Whittier, Longfellow and Hawthorne. Father had given her these, probably because to him she *was* a poem. Strangely, I do not know if she read them. I do know that in the first half of the twenties, she read and gave me Sigrid Undset's *The Bridal Wreath*, *The Mistress of Husaby*, and *The Cross*, which in 1929, under the title of *Kristin Lavransdatter*, won the Nobel Prize for Literature. This says a whole volume about her perceptions and tastes. One might elaborate here about the influence of such books. "All originality comes from reading," said the great botanist Julius von Sachs.

Father, a most ungypsy-like man because he did not wander, could, after a fifteen-hour day of toil, walk hand-in-hand with his young daughter, taking the milk cows to night pasture. From his six-foot-four height, with lifted head, he would seem to her even taller, as pointing, he said: "See how the wheel of stars turns on the hub of our hill!"

With the words I am writing here, I am taking you on what may be the last trip back to the Valley, the final exhumation of the Kristin-child in this book. Only after much contemplation is this happening set forth. I relate it here, but because of my mother's role, I would rather not return. Because of its far-reaching effects on my character it must be recounted, for this day, as well as my father's example in the acceptance of crosses, probably had more to do with my sense of worthiness as an adult than any other experience.

We go back:

Mother was often short on patience, and long on criticism. Neither Leo nor Kristin quite measured up to the standards of living she had known in Denmark and Wilmette. They were country kids.

Leo had a mind of his own and talked back. He was thirteen or fourteen at the time, not boyhood's most attractive age. Though Kristin was innovative, she was clumsy, which was not all due to having had polio. She evidenced no knack for home-making arts such as crocheting. She was unhandy. When she wrapped or tied anything, even her shoestrings, Mother often said, "You ought to be working in a gift shop some day." Though Kristin had not yet come upon the word *sarcasm*, she knew what Mother meant.

Mother admired perfection. That particular morning at breakfast, she had said what beautiful teeth Leo had: "So even and white, you should smile more than you do."

"Even when there's nothing to smile about?" he asked.

She ignored that. "Take good care of them. A pleasant smile is important."

Kristin's morning chores were finished and with Mother's permission, she was going down to the creek, first to fill a sorghum pail with sand to be mixed with garden loam for Mother's repotting of houseplants. Then maybe to catch some fish for supper.

She was sitting with her feet in shallow water, restoring her fishing net with newly-gathered willow saplings, when Leo came down with a team of horses to water. He looked moody and cross. "I never get time to do anything on my own. All I do is work, or school. Or sleep. I'm damn sick of it!"

"You eat, don't you? And quit swearing."

"Oh shut your goody-goody mouth!" he said, picking up a fair-sized tuft of sod and pitching it into the big burlap bag she was fitting with willow ribs. The muddied water splashed onto her face.

Something about the look she gave him made him ask, "I suppose you can hardly wait till you get to the house to tell on me?"

"No," she said, "but I just might tell what you and Laurence were going to do to Earl."

"Tattler, tattler, hanging on a bull's tail," he taunted.

"Well, I will tell about you boys locking the barn door on Mrs. Newton yesterday afternoon!" She could have held her tongue. It was Saturday and Grace was on the phone, already reporting this to Mother.

"Before you tell that, I just might drown you," he said, dropping the halter ropes and coming toward her.

She got to her feet, grabbed the little bucket of sand and fled up the incline to the house. As she ran, the pail swung back and forth.

Looking back, she saw how fast he was gaining on her. She let go of the pail and heard his sharp cry of pain. At the back porch, she saw what had happened. Blood poured from his mouth, and one of his beautiful front teeth dangled above his lower lip.

Mother at the kitchen window, still on the phone, caught the scene. She came out screaming, saw Leo holding the missile in the crook of his arm. She pointed to Kristin. He nodded his head. Mother went into a frenzy, first throttling, then crying and beating Kristin with her fists.

Father came running from the machine shed, grabbed the wash basin and threw water from a rain barrel in Mother's face, and her hysteria subsided. Leo was crying as much from fright as pain. "I tried to stop her. I said it was an accident and partly my fault. She wouldn't listen."

"She couldn't hear you," Father said. He took Kristin in one arm and held Leo close with his other. "Get a towel, wet it and press it hard against your mouth. Then can you get the car backed out of the garage?"

He soothed Kristin, washing her face and arms and lastly her dirty feet in cold water, without once looking at Mother.

"Can you go upstairs to your room? Will you lie on your bed and rest? I have to take your brother to the doctor and the dentist."

"Will I be all alone in the house?" she asked tremulously.

"You will not be alone. She will be downstairs," he said, looking now at Mother in such a way that Kristin remembered one of his sayings—Beware the impatience of a patient man!

Kristin got into her nightie and hung her wet dress on the back of a chair and lay down on her bed as Father said she should. The trembling did not stop for awhile, nor could she think clearly. The car went past the house with Father and Leo in it. There was quiet in the house. Maybe Mother was outside.

Kristin was less sorry for herself as reason returned. She thought about all the bad things she was guilty of —stealing raisins and brown sugar, blaming Albert for cutting her hair, and other fibs, peeking in the speller book during a test, killing Leo's turtle, laughing at Baba and Uncle Eric, not liking several town girls in catechism class and hating some of the Bible stories. How often she had deserved to be punished and was not? She had heard how other children got hard lickings at home. She was almost never spanked, only twice with the hairbrush. It all evened out and she was even sorry for Mother but more sorry about Leo's tooth. (She hadn't heard that half of the one next to it was broken off.) She fell asleep.

When she wakened, Mother was sitting beside the bed holding a glass of blackberry juice, her favorite. Kristin sat up to drink it. Mother said, "I'm so sorry! I lost control." Kristin lied and said, "I don't hurt anymore." They embraced, each of them forgiven.

Not so with Father. He had not been that serious and silent since the time he slept on the fur robes beside the couch when Kristin was five. Long after the bruises had faded, there was a kind of distance between Mother and him. And then the healing flesh closed it.

The unhappy over-worked woman whom Kristin became, punished her own children, sometimes rather harshly, and she almost never had the humility to say, "I'm sorry!" They forgave her and grew up, no longer children, and went their separate ways, and Howard, Richard, Kathleen, are no more. We are all human and imperfect and carry on in the ways set for us. For good or bad, I have long felt that self-incrimination, or contrition, is negative. How we use self-knowledge is important.

Mother was thirty-two when I was born, forty when Leo and I had the altercation beside the creek, which resulted in years of dental problems for Leo. In those days, women took "change of life" very seriously. There were the nostrums such as "Lydia Pinkham's Ladies' Tonics" and Doctor Worden's Female Pills."

Women, at this period in their lives, were supposed to faint and have hot flashes and be irrational. I decided to have no part in such histrionics. In family emergencies I was a Rock of Ages personified. And I never forgot that day, as I was lying on my bed and enumerating transgressions and figuring that somehow it all evens out in the long run. For such righteous self-control, I paid. And, I would have omitted this dark tale and glossed over others.

These are painful incidents, and I say that had I not read Loren Eiseley's *All the Strange Hours*, I might not have been heartened to excavate my own. This was the book he wrote when he knew his life was drawing to a close. He admonished that one must be wary, when pressed, in naming the writers who have influenced us. He warned that these admissions can cling to one as tenaciously as type-casting to an actor. Eiseley's pain-filled memories dwindle mine infinitesimally.

It seems that so much of my life, past and present, has revolved around the Valley. I know that too much of my shadow is there. I do keep returning, in memory and in the present. Much of my life, past and present, has the quality of *evernow*; it all seems of a piece. All these things influence my moments as they unfold.

I think of Rilke's words as I remember all those unforgotten people who have shared my life in the Valley. "Memory is not enough," he wrote. "One must be able to forget them when they are so many. Have patience to wait until they come again.

For it is not yet the memories themselves. Not till they have turned to blood within us, nameless and no longer to be distinguished from ourselves, not till then, can it happen that in a most rare hour, a verse arises and goes forth from these memories."

In the late 1960s, Reid Gilbert, born and raised in Appalachia, came to this area and founded the Wisconsin Mime Theatre and School, better known as The Valley Studio. The physical plant is still there under another name. The immediate environs of The Valley Studio years earlier had been the scene of the two tragedies retold in the poems "Wild Rose O'Neill" and "Where the Bittersweet Grew." Here took place the psychic experience detailed in "More Than Twice-Told Tales."

I am of the opinion that all these poems might not have "turned to blood with me" had I not been offered a relationship with that institution. There, during workshops I conducted, as I explained source material for poems, the students constantly urged that I dig deeper and deeper.

So I have been surrounded by a number of good friends in the Valley. There was Helen O'Brien, Youth Drama Specialist for the University of Wisconsin, who used my poems in performances and smaller readings, creating a larger audience for my work and making the poems seem much better. Such was her talent. Dale, her husband, encouraged me to be honest in my poems, to, as I wrote, set the record straight. And Reid Gilbert choreographed "The Round River Canticle" for television. Ever thus have gifted people given me a "hand up" and enriched my life. There have been many like the scholar, Father Brudermanns, who quite early had shared with me his unordinary library and culture.

What of the span from 1924 to 1960 and my first book of poems? Physical aspects of my life are partially summarized here and in the last chapter, called "Fascicle." But that is merely a glimpse of those years. I liken the first few to boot-camp; it was a training course for the real world. I survived, exchanging innocence and trust for experience. I would never again be so docile, so pliable.

In 1932—a fateful year, we skimped on everything but food to buy a Bosche console radio with a 12-inch dynamic speaker. No stereo or home-system has sounded so great, or filled such a need since. Our second good radio was a Stromberg-Carlson. They are like dear old friends and must be mentioned. They improved the quality of life.

WHA, "The Oldest Station in the Nation," was still young and I think of it as a sibling; we sort of grew together. One program shall serve as springboard here. Aired weekly, its opening text was this: "There is in the spring of our years a time for planting. Seed unsown in this time dies and brings forth no fruit, and the lands lie fallow. And the people yearn and go hungry in the season for harvest."

What glorious fare WHA provided for an isolated farm woman going about her work! There was music, reading, lectures. Soon there grew a correspondence with Ranger Mac, H.B. McCarty, Pops Gorden, Ray Stanley, Milton Bliss and others. For awhile I even did a five-minute stint called "A Farm Wife Reflects on Farm Life." Later, I was honored with a banquet as "Listener of the Year." WHA lecturers who come to mind from those years were Professors Philo Buck, Max Otto, David Fellman. I was material for molding.

And there was Father Dan, stopping between Madison and Dubuque each weekend, providing an oasis for discussion. How much of it was substantial? I felt this was the center of my life.

In 1945, my first poem was published and soon there were a few more. These were testing grounds for an early apprehension that a poem should have relevancy. The restraint in one's work, the ability to revise, should come as naturally to a poet as to a child, who, after pigging out on over rich food, concludes that a mending of ways is in order. Unfortunately, it seems not to be a lesson learned easily. I looked at some of my poems and remembered the over-conceived combing jacket at Edgewood that no one bought. Some of my early writings were that rococo.

My first training helped, and later, in writing courses I taught, I used one of these poems as an ice-breaker, telling the classes at the first session: "The author is in the room. Much as I might prefer not to, I am going to point out what is wrong with this poem, which is almost everything." After a couple of near-brutal criticisms, if a gasp was heard, I'd say, "If you are unable to take criticism, or to offer constructive suggestions, maybe you shouldn't be wasting your time and money in a poetry workshop?"

Which brings Robert E. Gard into our world. The century was at midpoint when he became the Man of the Hour in bringing participation in the arts to Wisconsin rural areas. Most of the emphasis then was on the first two syllables of the word *agri-culture*—county fairs to feature prize livestock and other produce, three-column picture stories about the Best. All of which was useful and proper.

Along came Professor Gard with fresh ideas for placing the accent on the last two syllables. The Rural Arts Association and The Wisconsin Regional Writers were his first two successful efforts. How eagerly he was welcomed cannot be adequately illustrated even by listing the subsequent groups he started.

I first saw him at a home-meeting in Mineral Point. Years later, he related a spooky experience he had, driving home over the road between Point and Dodgeville that night. How many communities he visited on these missions for the arts would be hard to estimate.

His First Lieutenant in these endeavors was a retired teacher and a writer, Fidelia Van Antwerp. Very early, she entered the friendship-circle and became a role model. Her enthusiasm was infectious and the sharing of herself phenomenal. Many of us thought she wore herself out in the cause, for she left us much too soon. Had it not been for the example set by "Fava" (as she was affectionately called) it is likely the Christopher Latham Sholes award would not have later been given to me. Fidelia was a pathfinder, as was Mary Zimmerman, her friend and mine, and Wisconsin's first and only poet laureate.

Add here the name of Louise Leighton, who founded the Wisconsin Fellowship of Poets, modeled after the New York Poetry Society and the League of Minnesota Poets, groups in which she had held offices. Here my love affair with WHA paid off. Production Manager Ray Stanley inaugurated a "Poet's Cor-

Robert Gard and Edna

ner" program, heard at 1:00 P.M. every Sunday for nearly three years. This brought known poets, and poetry people, out of closets, alleys, barnyards, into Wisconsin Fellowship membership. How well I know! having been its first secretary and second president.

One should not forget the many others who are worthy friends. There have literally been thousands of wonderful acquaintances, about a hundred of whom have left their marks in unforgetable incidents of kindness, inspiration and loyalty.

Thinking on them, poets and writer-friends, past and present, I call on Emily's words to encompass them with what I cannot:

The sweeping up the heart, and putting love away,
We shall not want to use again until eternity.

Like windsongs over summer meadows, many of my associations were with younger people, stemming from the Rhinelander School of the Arts, the flowering of another Robert Gard idea.

He saw in some of us potential of which we were unaware. I had, for instance, never thought of myself as a teacher. He brought to Rhinelander, Wisconsin, nationally known writers: Gwendolyn Brooks, Archibald Macleish, Marc Connolly, A.B. Guthrie, Jesse Stuart, Studs Terkel, Hoke Norris, William Stafford, Max Golightly, Robert Bly, Harry Mark Petrakis, and Wisconsin's own August Derleth and Herbert Kubly. With some of these people, brief correspondences ensued.

Herb Kubly, for one, had won the National Book Award. We had not met in those days, though I read his books. *Varieties of Love*, a collection of his short stories, has been ranked by critics with the best of American literature. A lasting friendship developed. He may not have been the first to suggest the possibilities of the present work, but he was the first to go on record:

> My hope is that she will transpose her rich life into art with an autobiographical prose-poetry book, a prose narrative of her life in which she would be candid, witty and wise, interspersed with poems when they fit into the narrative. She has promised me that she will do this and I know that such a book will be a richly human success with an appeal to the contemporary woman.

Once, during those mid-century years, returning from a Milwaukee writer's meeting, I was stranded in Hill's Coffee Shop off the Square. This was also the first Greyhound depot in Madison.

The bus-drivers were waiting for a blizzard to subside. At the lunch counter an older gentleman, wearing a pea coat and sailor's stocking cap, made opening talk. At his suggestion, we went to a small table. He removed the cap and I was struck by his appearance. His was the face of a scholar as truly as "The Thinker" represents what it does. He even looked like the Rodin sculpture, "Thought." We talked for several hours. I liked his name, Lee Douglas. At home, I told Father Dan and Peter, "Today I have met either a genuine genius or a real-life Walter Mitty."

Ours became almost entirely a friendship-by-mail. Somewhere in this home are hundreds of letters, many of which deserve publication. He was a poet who never published, a violinist who gave up performing, a designer, a mathematician. One of his classmates at University of Wisconsin was Kenneth Fearing. He was a pantheist who fancied himself an atheist. He was drunk on symbolism and turned me to free verse. Though his own poetry lacked restraint, I learned a lot from him about criticism—what to accept, what to reject.

Lee Douglas, *not* my brother Leo, is the make-believe "Uncle Paul" in the short story "Yesterdays." He has a role in my novel, *A Headstone for Jules*, if I live to finish it. Where is he now? His last letter arrived the day after his death, in 1973. This is what he said, among other things: "I think that finally I've turned conventional mathematics inside out, solved problems about Time waiting to be worked out for more than twenty-five hundred years." Where are those papers? They *were* in a footlocker at Wood Veteran's Home waiting flames, or shredder.

Later, I wrote a poem for him, called "Safari," a few lines of which I relate:

Big game falls to the Huntress this November-day:
You and Ezra Pound (of a kind with Voltaire).
Your defense of his right to be wrong dimensioned me.
. . . More than for mind programmed to infinitude
I mourn what it was in you that infused me
with liking for heresies, mistrust of Truths,
to anticipate sharp teeth in Beauty's smile.
. . . Teacher! We shall die knowing too late
the slurred syllables for what we meant. . . .

Which brings us back to the statement of Julius von Sach I quoted at the beginning: "All originality comes from reading." Like most so-called 'truths' it is only partly true. Now and then we can speak for ourselves and state what it true. For interviews or Who's Who publications I have said or written: "Formally, I am an uneducated woman. But I have been exposed in my associations to more learning than anyone has a right to have known." The publisher of my first poetry volume wrote, "She is a poet of striking originality in both thought and style." If this is true, it came no more from reading than from entrance into the Old World culture of Father Brudermanns; the society of Dominican nuns; the life of Father Dan, teacher of Latin, Greek and History; the mind of friend Lee Douglas; others unnamed and yet to be named.

Perhaps all of this is background to the central occurence of my life. I know that all events flow into or out of it. What happened on April 20, 1959 at 10:15 P.M. was not of the life of the mind, nor perhaps of the physical world.

It was then that I came to full understanding of lines written by one of those philosophers, the dramatist Aristophanes:

Each of us is a torn half whose lost
other we keep seeking across time.

At this time Father Dan was serving as part-time chaplain at St. Joseph's Hospital less than two miles away from our home. After having officiated at Benediction for the Franciscan Sisters, and making his rounds to the critically ill, he drove back to our farm. And after that:

No more coming down a darkness road, at the door
your ashen face luminous for being safely home,
your bloodless hands in mine to warm. . . .

Proudly I escorted him to see the new drapes I'd hung in his freshly-papered room. No one else could express appreciation with such grace and sincerity as he.

Leaving the room, we came to the piano which he grasped suddenly. I was behind him with my three-year-old grandson between us. Half turning, he pushed the child to one side as he fell in coronary occlusion. His two final words on this earth were the child's name, "Christopher! Christopher!" which means *Christ Bearer.* It will ever be a word, a name, of special significance to me, though generally-styled "theologians" have demoted this patron of travellers from sainthood.

I was no stranger to grief, having lost children, father, mother, my dearest friend from Edgewood to suicide, a beloved Aunt Julia. There were others from whom partings were near-sorrows. I loved Father Dan more than anyone else, more than life itself, I think. I needn't have told him. He knew. He may have doubted when I said, "As long as life, I will love you!" Not all things remain true. This one has.

I told myself then that I would never write again, false words, as it turned out. Five months later, on September 14, my natal day, almost as if full realization had not come till then (he had always made so much of the occasion) I wrote the "Round River Canticle" —all nine parts of the poem, in longhand. It was "given" to me, an inspired poem.

Basically it remains as written, though tightened in places. The floodgates were open that day. Then I wrote so much that before the winter ended, and adding previously published ones, there were enough poems for a book.

Rosily I sent it off to a Catholic publishing house in New York. It was a manuscript rich in spirituality. It was not religious verse. Imagine my shock when it came back with a cranky letter from the senior editor. Its gist was that no one is publishing such idealistic material. He wrote that "In this gravelly age, no one will believe your relationship with the priest."

A nerve had been found, or else all sensitivity had perished in his pulpit. I was crushed and decided to never send the manuscript out again. So much for good resolutions!

A few months later, rummaging in some papers, I came across a copy of *The Country Poet,* where my poem "Neighbor" had appeared. The editor-publisher, Edwin P. Geauque, had written me a warm letter, his words full of praise for my work. Now hope and reason prevailed. The New York experience was

*Edna and grandson Chris (*Mineral Point Democrat *photo)*

only one man's opinion. This publisher lived in the White Mountains of New Hampshire. He liked the nature of my work.

Once again, I sent off my manuscript. *The Round River Canticle* was published in 1960. It won a national first prize, as did two individual poems in the volume. The sponsors received their copies, and it was favorably reviewed. Ray Stanley gave it a magnificient reading, with commentary, over WHA. But I was disappointed that the book did not sell well in Wisconsin.

Edwin Geauque is one of those friends whose faith in me appears to me boundless. I can never repay him for all the kindness and support. I consider the finely-handcrafted books he has produced masterworks in this age of mass production; they enhance the contents considerably. Though we have never met, our correspondence is voluminous and revelatory.

Again, the turn of earthly years waxed and waned. It is not that *love* wanes. It widens its wings and flies on pinions beyond our sight. And we grow gray, who breathe in disappointments and loneliness; we try to believe we will all meet again, though not here in these broken years. I gather up the shards, as Mother did the broken cover of the rose jar. I would hold these together with an amalgam of duty and the amenities, lesser affections and human respect.

I stepped out of the shower late one afternoon in June 1962, to answer the phone. The call was from Cleveland, Ohio, where the National Federation of State Poetry Societies (hereafter referred to as NFSPS) was holding its fourth annual convention. Would I consider the presidency?

Out the window could be seen Christopher, perched in the crotch of a cedar tree, wearing a high feathered headdress—a young brave who would start school in the fall. Why not, I thought! We'd already been to Louisiana and Texas on speaking engagements. We'll go to conventions and see America together! "Yes," I said, "if the consensus is that I'm capable."

I had never been to their conventions. Their sole appraisal or consideration of me was based on action I'd taken when president of the Wisconsin Poets Fellowship, maneuvering our state society into becoming a charter member of the NFSPS. That was a ploy less out of foresight, or faith in the goals of the new organization, than from dissatisfaction with the then-current situation in poetry circles. The mid-American writers were not simply being ignored by the East and far-West; apparently they did not know we existed.

I had simply said yes, and then forgot the NFSPS. That is until March when letters began coming, and a copy of a news release was sent to State newspapers. The letters were inquiries as to what I was planning for the 1963 convention to be held in Madison? If ever I needed a panic button! Either the secretary at the Cleveland meeting had failed to send the minutes and accumulated records, or had misssent them, whatever. I was in deep water.

Much of my life has been characterized by caution, as if some invisible guardian were warning me to take care! I didn't always hear, or maybe the clamor of living rendered it impossible; some call it a sixth sense, some ESP. Son Richard called his a "built-in-clock." We could awaken at any specified hour, meet obligations on time without consulting a calendar and so forth. In what may have been a period of gestation, for nearly nine months, obviously mine was out of commission.

This is the sort of thing that was happening to me: soon after the phone call from the NFSPS convention, I had a close call. Our siamese cat had delivered herself of kittens which no one had been able to find. Lunch was over, the men were in the fields, Chris was supposed to be taking a nap because we had tickets to see Robert Preston live in *The Music Man* at the Orpheum Theatre in Madison that evening.

I decided to climb up into the haymow to look for the kittens. From the ladder, I'd gone only a few yards when I fell into a pocket between the bales of hay. In this method of storage, the bales were placed on a movable elevator and tossed at random into the loft. Had I fallen to the bottom, I might have been a mysterious disappearance. I recalled the skeleton in the quarry.

I was only ten or twelve feet down, both my arms pinioned straight above by solid bales. There was a lot of pain in my right shoulder, and I did not know if they were baling in the fields. Easing shoes off, I prayed, and all the while, toe over toe, inched myself to the top. Except that the hay was coarse and rough, it was like a birth canal and I, free, born again.

Coming down the ladder, I knew the shoulder was broken. I also knew that shoulders cannot be set. In the house I took an aspirin and a hot bath. My arms, bare during the falling and climb, looked like a map of the populous East printed in red. I coated them well with zinc stearate powder and put on a long-sleeved blouse. Figuring one may as well be entertained while hurting, as sitting at home, we saw *The Music Man* that evening. Thus, as usual, bodily hurts were given short shrift. But never so the mind and migraines!

But with all this, there was a national convention to be planned by a woman who was raising a young grandchild, who could not drive, and whose husband had little empathy with her outside activities. Sure, one could write letters and find out details, but how make the arrangements? Insomnia, that faithful companion, made frequent visitation. Spring equinox, Mother's natal day, came and went. Silently I pleaded with other ancestors. No response, and then another strange phone call.

Louise Marsden was Society Editor of Madison Newspapers. We had met only once at an awards banquet.

"What are you doing about that poetry convention?" she asked in her warm, all-encompassing voice. She had read the release and was wondering why nothing was forthcoming from the NFSPS president.

"Nothing yet," I said, and explained my predicament. She said nothing for about a minute, then, "I've someone in mind who would make a great convention chairman. I'm having lunch with him on Saturday at the Hoffman House. Could you come in and join us?"

Do the drowning grasp for support? Was Greyhound in the bus business?

John M. Grinde did not arrive on-the-minute. "He was a classmate," Louise said, "You'll find he's not ordinary. But he's brilliant, first in his class at medical school. And he writes poetry."

He arrived, affable and enthusiastic. Not only did he put his wheels at my disposal, but his talents and money as well.

He sent out, literally, hundreds of letters which brought such people as Ralph Purcell, the personal representative of Roger Stevens, executive director of the National Endowment for the Arts; two New York publishers; editors of several respectable poetry magazines. Headquarters were the Madison Inn, and the Wisconsin Center. The Starlight Roof or the Ballroom were for socializing.

Dr. Grinde knew Aaron Bohrod, who exhibited his work. Professor Fred Buerki, director of the Union Theatre, addressed us, as did Helen C. White. At considerable personal expense, Grinde brought Henry Rago, editor of *Poetry Magazine*, to address us. August Derleth, ever the supportive friend, came for much less.

For the first time, there were real, printed programs, as well as some offbeat things. Dr. Grinde rigged a colored strobe light to one side at the back of the stage. "To keep the audience awake," he said. To keep the speakers alert, he had at two main sessions four large fellows dressed in black suits and hats, with arms folded across their chests, sitting in the front row.

In 1971, the National Federation again convened in Madison, hosted by Wisconsin Fellowship of Poets and Edgewood College. I was the convention chair who invited William Stafford, then Poetry Consultant to the Library of Congress, to be our featured poet. He brought his wife, Dorothy, and two of their children. He was more like an old friend to us than a celebrity.

Attendance was sizable, the setting and weather ideal. Dr. and Mrs. Grinde attended several sessions. But the cast had changed; only a few remembered him. In his memory, I've detailed that prior convention, to set the record in place. And August Derleth, who as the newly-designated Honorary Chancellor of NFSPS, gave the main address, "My Life in Poetry." It was a summation written especially for the occasion. This was his final public appearance.

There is another exception to Loren Eiseley's advice to be wary of naming writers to whom we are indebted. I take you

Last photo of August Derleth, taken in Edna's backyard, June 15, 1971 (Dale O'Brien Photo)

back in time to April 7, 1935, to a radio broadcast, I think it was WMAQ, Chicago, in a program from New York, a tribute to Edwin Arlington Robinson who had died the day before. The first announcer said that Robinson worked on the revisions of his booklength poem *King Jasper* "right up to the end." Poet Ridgely Torrance read the wonderful "Carmichael" sonnet from *Captain Craig*, then Ben Ray Redman read what I took to be all of *The Man Against the Sky*. I was spellbound as the poem went on.

Even then I still hoped, if ever there was time, to write fiction. I was only twenty-nine and entertained the usual romantic notions. Sentiment lingered on. But this was revelation! Maybe it was thus with Saint Paul, horseback on the road to Damascus? I could as reasonably have fallen out of the chair. The poem ended and then it was Torrance's melancholy voice, I think. He closed the broadcast with this reminiscence: "Once Robinson was criticized for his philosophy of life. 'Robinson is a pessimist,' it was said. 'He writes of life as if it were a prison.' To which he replied sadly, 'No, not a prison but a kindergarten, in which all are trying to spell G O D with the wrong blocks.' "

We had, at the time, our first traveling library service. I ordered every Robinson book available. Studying, I copied pages on pages, until a composition notebook was filled in longhand. Today I would offer here an educated opinion —having read everything written by all three. It may be that only Shakespeare, with Alexander Pope a close second, have left more quotable epigrams that Robinson. Yet other than the much anthologized poems, few of today's readers know his work—though Robinson influenced some of the poets people do study. It might be said that Robinson was one of our first subsidized writers.

President Theodore Roosevelt, after reading *The Children of the Night*, created a job for him in the U.S. Customs Office. Robinson was too proud to accept "charity." (Today we call it a "grant.") Robinson was the first to receive three Pulitzer Prizes, as well as most of our nation's highest literary honors, yet there has never been issued for him a commemorative postage stamp. Is this an oversight? Hardly. The NFSPS has requested this with letters and full petitions. In this, he is like the artist Camille

Pisarro, sometimes called the Father of Impressionism, but eclipsed by those who copied his style. Here we might let Walt Whitman have his say:

> He that by me spreads a wider breast than my own,
> proves the width of my own;
> He most honors my style who learns under it to destroy
> the teacher.

I don't believe it! There's a lot of "Richard Cory" in Whitman. He glitters when he talks.

Oh, it is true, Robinson wrote too much. His collected works fill fifteen-hundred pages. His lines are often merely naturalistic prose. There will be some reading these words who also know Robinson and they may be puzzled that his influence was so strong upon me:

My poetry is a kind of transcription of personal experience. Robinson almost never drew from his life, but of those opposite from his own in every level of society, from the most pitiable to the most envied. Critics have said that his was a life of fantasy, because he never married, and for other reasons which critics find. I think he was possessed by anquish and secrets of the soul. He wrote his characters as he saw them.

And that was what made him, that first day of my discovery, a kind of poet-god. I had not yet accepted that life was, in a sense, a trial by water-wheel, not an equal ration of air and water, joy and sorrow, but I suffered then from anemia and overwork. The romantic, memorized poems no longer had value and I was nearly ten years away from discovery of T. S. Eliot's *Four Quartets* and its, for me, memorable passages such as "Humankind cannot stand too much reality."

These days there is revived interest in Pisarro. He is surfacing in books and an occasional exhibit. Maybe Robinson's prophecy will come true and literature be closer to full circle in the fulfillment of his: "I shall have more to say when I am dead."

I have admitted to his long-windedness and a waning of enthusiasm because of it. Of this, returning to favorite poems, he was always forgiven. And there are few poems to which I relate more fervently that to his magnificent *Tristram*, more poignantly, that those spoken by King Howel to his daughter, Isolt:

> Thank God, my child
> that I was wise enough never to thwart you
> when you were never a child. If that was wisdom
> say on my tomb that I was a wise man.

Father Dan

There were times during their late years when Fannie was moved to say to her husband, Justice O.W. Holmes: "Why is your handsomeness enhanced by age, while I only grow less attractive?" Perhaps one feels this way about loved ones.

Even in his coffin one could not fail to be struck by the way suffering had refined Father Dan's good looks to beauty. I recall coming into the funeral home that first time, after he was finally taken from our home. Archbishop Binz, who had visited him nearly every month during the four years he was here, was standing beside the casket looking puzzled: "What is it? Why doesn't he look like Dan?"

The mortician, Bill Gorgen, said "I did my best. We were good friends. I did not alter his features, Your Excellence."

Probably neither of the men had ever seen him without glasses. Father Dan had damaged his eyesight in the seminary. (How else is one to attain all "A"s in Latin, Greek, Medieval History, Advanced Rhetoric and related subjects!) Anticipating their reactions, I had brought his horn rimmed glasses and fitted them to his face.

"He has no need of these but maybe others do." On this day, it was an inane remark. "Yes, Yes," they nodded, appreciative.

Father Daniel P. Coyne

The next morning there was a Solemn Requiem Mass at St. Paul's in Mineral Point for area people. For twenty-one years throughout southwestern Wisconsin, Father Dan had been a substitute pastor, on weekends, during pastoral vacations and holidays. And the day following, two such Masses were offered in Dubuque. The early one was at Loras College, the second at the archdiocesan cathedral downtown.

During these days especially, I did not sleep well. I am a poor sleeper in general and I particularly do not sleep well away from home. Hotels are the most challenging—good reason to forego extensive travel. The Julien in Dubuque provided a room with a view to the black, star-cluttered sky for the first of those ordeals by anguish.

There were memories out there into which I need plunge, treacherous as the Great River that rolled past the hotel. Torn strands of dreams and lost living to be woven into what kind of fabric, I knew not. It was three nights before that I had met him at our door. He was ashen faced, returning from hospital duty. It was a far ways back to the day of our first meeting on this earth:

I had been bedridden after the birth of my first child, Richard, in late June of 1925. In those days, it was the only way to control hemorrhaging. The day before he was born, the brothers of two of my best friends at Edgewood were ordained in Madison. What has not changed throughout my life is my sense of decorum regarding the late stages of pregnancy. I've never felt it a good practice to make childbirth a family spectacle.

It was in late August when Father Dan and I met. When the noon meal was over on this day, I fed the baby and put him in his crib, tightly covered with netting to ward off the ever-present housefly. Richard would sleep a full two hours. It had rained that morning, so I went out immediately to pull weeds in the neglected garden and to find vegetables for our supper. Hurting breasts told the time to go in.

Grimy and disheveled, I was latching the garden gate when a car came into the yard. My friend from Edgewood Anna Coyne and two young men got out. Oh, I knew who they were!

My bare feet were muddy and I was wearing only an old cotton housedress and a panty. The temperature was in the nineties. The entry to the house was through the kitchen, where flies had congregated on the unwashed dishes. The baby was crying his double needs. Bending to change him, I was aware that my sweaty dress was clinging and that my breasts, responding to his cries, were dripping. At no time, before or since, has embarrassment been so acute. There was no escaping this ugly scene—only an insecurity akin to shame.

Many years later the men told me that their response was the opposite of mine. To them I was like a living Madonna. Burping the cherubic baby, I was enveloped in a kind of aura they took to be modesty, not shame. Father Dan said, "You were lovely as a painting by Ribero, with your great shadowed eyes." Ah yes, anemia.

During the next seven years we would meet only once and from that second encounter one remark only remains: "Out in the country, what do you and Peter do for amusement?" I was offended and did not reply, disappointed in a man I longed to know. It was a query to haunt us in the future, when being in each other's company was the main ingredient for happiness.

In the darkness before dawn at the Julien Hotel, there were few continuous recollections, little urgency. A few days before, I would have gone silently to a door, listening for his breathing. I had always expected he would slip away in sleep, as had Mother. Now I thought only of girding myself for the coming day: hundreds of his fellow priests to be faced, men who, when it seemed he might live awhile after the double infarct, banded together and bought a fine television set to lighten his days.

Most of these visitors had come to our home at least once, some regularly, such as Msgr. George Stemm, Don Ameche's first drama mentor. (Ameche came twice.) Stemm had sent out the call for the TV donors. And Msgr. Vernon Peters, one of Iowa's notable ham radio operators, came on a blustery December day and installed the roof antenna and whatever else was necessary to insure good reception. There were others, for Father Dan had classmate friends in five colleges and universities.

It had been an open house for years. Athletic celebrities: Arch Ward and Elmer Layden and their contemporaries may not register with today's readers—fame, so fleeting! In the guarding of privacy, no word of such visitors appeared in the local paper, where from time to time a long distance call to a parent was newsworthy. The editor was Ed Mundy, who each week had an interesting feature column, *The Pick-Up-Man*.

On May 8, 1952, this item: "The old Grace farm, owned for a few years by Sam Murrish, is now owned by Mr. and Mrs. Peter Meudt and is a haven for tired clergy. The Rev. Lloyd Glass, M.M., long-time missionary in China, who spent many months in prison camps, finds retreat here after countless speaking engagements. He was out this day driving a tractor and thoroughly enjoying this diversion from mental effort, as well as the beautiful highground view. His mother, Mrs. Albert Glass, of Cresco, Iowa, was also a guest in the home. Another guest was the familiar Father Dan Coyne of Dubuque, former athletic coach and director of public relations at Loras College. He was trying his hand at repairing a screen door and received the commendation of the caller for engaging in honest toil." There was more, about me, which ended with a line for which I am forever indebted to Mr. Mundy: "Her poetry indicates an unusually deep and appreciative mind."

The riches of those shared friendships were overwhelming: men from Gate of Heaven Leprosarium in China, priests from the Philippines, South America, Africa. There was even a sportscaster, then known as "Dutch" Reagan. Through Father Dan, the world was at our door. So many thousands of memories.

But this day, I girded myself and set forth without him. *Dies irae, dies illa*!

That afternoon I rode in the hearse with Bill Gorgen to Madison, where there would be visitation and the final Requiem at St. Raphael's Cathedral the next day. This was Father Dan's last trip. In his studies and work, when he first recruited students and accompanied athletic teams, when he was college official and then contract chaplain for Midwest U.S. Forces in World War II, during parish services and the conducting of retreats, he had probably driven more than a million miles.

We were on West Washington Avenue. I said to Bill, "Tomorrow, from here to Resurrection Cemetery will mark the end of his travels here. For me this is the last mile with him. Humor me and drive around the Capitol Square."

When we came to Woldenberg's Clothiers, I asked him to slow down. "A month ago I bought this coat I'm wearing in that store. Father Dan was with me." It was a navy blue cashmere.

Bill said, "When Gladys took it to hang up the other evening, she remarked how luxurious and light it is."

"Yes, for my style, an extravagance. I've never bought things like that. Over a hundred dollars for a cloth coat, on a half-price sale! I told Father Dan that the function of a coat was for warmth and I could do without it."

"What changed your mind?" Bill asked.

"Not so much *what* as *who*. He said, 'I know you can do without. But buy it to honor me.' I was so accustomed to having him near, so used to his often cryptic statements, that its significance was lost on me."

"But how could you have known?"

"Because I could see what was happening in him. The store was warm. He removed his overcoat and asked for a chair. He sat with his left hand under his left armpit and against his ribs as if to subdue the pounding of a worn-out heart."

"Yes, how he held himself was indicative of the condition. But only the double-jointed can maneuver that, another reason he was such a fine athlete." After a silence, he asked: "Did you never worry about a coronary occlusion when you were riding with him?"

"Never. But I worried when he drove alone."

After dinner with the relatives and the public visitation, the sanctuary of a room in the Park Hotel. Sadly, I looked out the window to the cathedral where he had attended school, been an altar boy and offered his first Mass. Everything I was seeing reminded me that for the several weeks when I was a little girl, I had stayed on Milton Street, near him.

He had grown to be the pride of his family, his teachers, his parish. He had been chosen and appointed secretary to Archbishop Kane of Dubuque, a position that ordinarily promised successive honors in the Church. And it was a period when Holy Orders held a certain glamor for some, as similarly, entertainers or sports figures lived for their followings.

I was simply grieving, not searching for answers. And that may be one reason why I was given that night to wondering. Why had I met this man, work-worn, disadvantaged young farm woman that I was? The two cities in which he lived were full of pretty girls and women who would have welcomed his attention, and maybe more.

His mother, Regina, entered my thoughts. Rememberings took on new meanings. On the day of my marriage, as if in presentiment, she (in Madison) had cried most of the time, while I was in Wyoming Valley, Spring Green and enroute to Tomah. During the Edgewood years a mutual fondness developed between us. When I was told of her weeping that whole day, the daughter explained: "It was because you were so young."

Sharply, Mrs. Coyne had objected: "I don't know the reason. How can you know?"

Now I wondered if she had wept at his ordination, seeing him prostrate and face down before the altar, renouncing the world and its pleasures. Had she misgivings along with her pride in his powers and achievements? I had to settle for what was known. The bond between mother and son had been special and strong.

Another son, William, two years older than Father Dan, died at Creighton University, the result of a football injury. He was nearly twenty, also studying for the priesthood. These two brothers had been inseparable, as my two sons had been. Dan's older brothers, Thomas and John, had wives, James was in high school, Anna in the grades.

Regina Coyne's life had been marked by tragedy and extreme hardship. While she was carrying Anna, her husband was killed in an accident, during which she also was badly injured. Five young sons to feed and cloth, very little money. No Aid to Dependent Children then. It was the worst of times. I still suspect that those early years of long paper routes for Dan Coyne, truck gardening, odd jobs, may have contributed to his weakened heart.

For the rest of that night, until fitful sleep came, I tried to concentrate on happy times, on all the firsts he had brought into our rural lives. Externals, yes, but important to family maturity. Firsts, from the mundane to the majestic: holiday turkeys, a turntable and then recordings, a typewriter.

There were excursions to great cities for World's Fairs and art galleries and plays. In Washington D.C., *Knickerbocker Holiday* ("Oh, the days dwindle down when you reach September / And it's a long, long way from May to December") New York and *Oklahoma* ("People will say we're in love"). Trips to cattle congresses and the Corn Palace; spiritual pilgrimages to Gettysburg, to the acres of white crosses at Arlington and Baton Rouge.

He was with me for the partings from Howard, Father and Mother.

I wakened to bright sunlight, having nearly overslept.

Where was Peter during those three days? Though he was actively farming, he joined me at the services in Mineral Point, Dubuque and Madison. He stood with his hand to my elbow in Resurrection Cemetery. These were his gestures of respect, demonstrations of our relationship, as difficult as it might have been for him. On the way home to Dodgeville, we spoke but little. I did thank him for his support. And I said, "A lot of angers have been canceled." I prepared a good supper. Later, asleep, I did not hear him come in after the evening chores.

I have been frequently asked, mostly by writer friends, about the name "Meudt." Why is it pronounced "Might?" Why hadn't it been corrected? To which there was a stock reply: "The first Peter Meudt served in the Civil War. He and his wife, Mary, had fourteen children, eight of whom were sons who had remained in this community." Another question: Why, for literary purposes had I not used my maiden name? For that, no stock response. I may never have explained till now, though it is hinted at in my poem "Anniversary."

The poet Robert Frost could be articulate about unrequited love. Peter suffered it in silence or anger. It may well be that the silences he inflicted on others had their source in this pain. Was I unaware? Hardly. In all the lifetime settlings of second-bests on others, there must be guilt. My burden was lightened when there was an award, a recognition, or well-published piece, as if it were recompense for being wife in name only.

I was entering a period that can only be described as a sense of abandonment—a season of death-wishes when I found comfort in the obituaries of persons my age or younger. Had someone suggested then that someday I might be writing about this, I would have been incredulous. Today, putting this chapter into words I realize it could nearly fill a book. Unlike Megan in the *Thornbirds*, I was not jealous of God, my need was not for vengeance.

When close friends say: "Now, with the new freedoms, you might well have married. Isn't it frustrating for you?" To which I generally reply: "If I was wise enough then not to want God as a rival, I should be so foolish now?" What I did not explain was that there was no conflict. My own leanings were toward the religious life. (I acknowledge that I may not have been well suited to it.) There had been my child-love, Father Brudermanns. Add to that a Christ-like element in Father Dan. Had he proposed apostasy, I might have loved him less.

One thing remains to be told about an occurence which happened four months after Father Dan's passing. As in the year of our first meeting, it was late August. I wakened that morning to find on the nightstand a slip of paper. In Father Dan's handwriting, this quotation:

> "Beloved I will send my angel before you to keep you in your journey." *Exodus 23*

I had never seen it before, though I knew he wrote out such notes before addressing groups. Perhaps in trepidation, I have never sought its source. I share the occurence to comfort the sorrowful. It was as if he had come home from a flight too far to fathom, becoming a presence to be called on from that hour to now.

A few years later, James A. Pike, previously an Episcopal Bishop, would tell of similar phenomenon. Much was made of this in September of 1969, when he perished in a Judean desert, and then was denounced as a charlatan or a psychotic. I was diminished by the report. I went to Edwin Arlington Robinson and reread sections of "Amaranth." Coming to the lines I was seeking, the book could be put aside:

> We are too brisk
> In our assumption of lightness
> Under a burden we have never felt,
> And too remiss in calling ourselves liars
> For saying well so much more than we know.

More than twenty-eight years have passed since that scrap of paper on the nightstand. To this day, I cannot know whether it was Morning Star or Vesper. It did mark an end to the morbid scanning of obituaries. The facade of interest in family and friends fell away for renewed caring. I began to think about writing again.

These days science runs amuck in the cosmos; it lays a heavy hand on my intelligence and humor with its theories about the universe. Is is circular? A black hole? A sponge-like formation?

Today when Love has tarnished, or is seemingly without identity, I cannot recapture what truly happened after the twenty-sixth year of my life, except to imagine I was like Eve seeing fire for the first time. Mystery beyond human comprehension, its power and potential, which if understood, few might choose to bear.

But I still believe that only through incandescence of this nature, can fire again be made our minister to sustain or destroy, so that in its going out and afterglow, we enter the corridors of another universe. It is the universe of the spirit. Or call it . . . the universe of God.

Fascicle

It must seem to many we are on the verge of another war. I mark with wonder those other times of calamity, how during World War I people drew closer in communities, and how in the Forties War they still found comfort in personal communication. Now, served by the media as we are, it has lost meaning. Everyone is informed. All have the questions for every ill and there is not even God to ask for an answer?

Now and then I dream of old neighbors, of Nora, Julia, Emma, Austin, Nels, of my brother, Leo—strange, straggling dreams without continuity or rational content: of incidents that I have not stored away in some drawer, for storing indicates order, but more as if these have lain like old artifacts and appliances in a memory-dump. Often as not I waken in tears and am then sleepless from a kind of feverish inner vision as though I've seen a disconcerting film of my own being. It is there in microcosm, the hurrying through eighty-one earthly years, stumbling over the stones, whenever possible stepping back from confrontation, taking cover from threatening storm.

Yet mostly failing in these ploys I met with anguish and care, my wilful, earthbound spirit caught reflections of spiritual intervention. Sometimes it has been like living in a presence that has sheathed me from basal fear, from possessiveness, from most problems born of human pride. I have always been incapable of hatred, or holding a grudge, of being judgemental or mean. Sanctimonious as this may sound, it is true. And the pity is that I deserve no credit. It may quite simply mean a lack in character, or, more constructively, my father's Bohemian Gypsy genes. We are as we are. Goethe said: "Man's soul is his fate."

As I write this, April is here again—month for assassinations and brewing of wars, conversely of resurrection and opening buds. Until man tampered with the order of nature it was the month of birth. I sit on the wrap-around porch looking on scenes much as I wrote about in sunshine and a strong wind—always the wind blows in this Upland—so unlike the Valley where high hills robbed hours of light from each day. Here, too, meadowlands fall away to the east, but to the west is the cherished cowl-like horizon I have described in many poems. I have just stated a lack of angers. This in no way relieves one of vivid recall.

I moved as a bride to a large rented farm on Pleasant Ridge, into a situation ravaged by the death in Dodgeville of Peter's mother. There were plans and an option to buy. My in-laws Frank and Ellen had married when she was forty. They had been engaged and had quarreled eighteen years before. To this late union two sons were born: Peter and his brother William. Ellen was a seamstress, a flawless homemaker. Each night Frank cleaned the kitchen range and precisely laid kindling for the morning fire. He was a bitter old man (because of the wasted years, I thought) and should not have been expected to welcome me into that household: father, two sons and a hired man.

I was early October, 1924. I was three months out of boarding school. Within a year Richard was born at home, likewise Howard, one year later. During that pregnancy, Peter broke his leg in two places. Fourteen months later his arm was broken backwards at the elbow. During months-long therapy to regain some use of the arm, he developed psoriasis—an hereditary affliction.

During all of this I carried well-water for heating to launder the clothes with washboard and tubs. When necessary or when able, I helped with the milking. Because town was eight miles distant and the budget was tight, I gardened. None of the men ever helped. I suffered miscarriages and survived and was unhappy. I could not know I was being tempered and tried for a relationship as lasting and as devastatingly memorable as those read about in Father Brudermann's books—when I was a child weeping over Dante and Evangeline.

Frank Meudt died during the second year of the depression, and the farm owner, out of a job, left the city to take up farming. Frank had invested money in two other farms but neither Peter nor William could gain possession because of the economy, bank failure and moratorium. An interim of three years was spent at subsistence level on a rundown place. It is the site of the poem with which this book ends.

We came here—to this wrap-around porch —Peter, Richard, Howard, Kathleen and I, in 1936. The abstract informed that the farmstead was laid out by a Jones family. It is land once owned by Henry Dodge, Wisconsin's first governor and senator. His homesite is a very short distance, as the hawk flies, from where I sit. This is a substantial, fine house, built in the 1850s. It four-room basement walls are of stone three feet thick. Behind it then was a huge overland barn that sheltered cattle, horses and sheep. Close by was a machine shed and henhouse. Nearer the house was the windmill that pumped water to a large concrete stock tank. To the east and south a few rods ran a creek in a gentle valley. It was so beautiful, bordered as it is by Governor Dodge Woods and an incredible expanse folding into hills, that even though it was March first, cold and barren, I fell in love with it, with the whole scene. Further south on high ground, running diagonally across a field, was our private road to the main highway. In winter storms, the wind kept it passably bare.

The farm had been in the hands of speculators: a banker and a physician. It was one of the two on which Frank held the mortgate during a bad time for all. The two men were property-poor, desperate to raise tax money. One year they stripped the pasture of virgin walnut trees, another year they sold forty acres next to the buildings. There were other shenanigans on the part of the banker, who suffered a nervous breakdown. The doctor, who had delivered my children and who had twice made night calls to stanch my hemorrhaging (the Rh factor being an unknown) committed suicide. The meadows are fields now and the pasture overgrown with hawthorn.

We lost Howard in 1936 as a result of misdiagnosed appendicitis. It was the day before Thanksgiving and the doctor was careless and hurried. He gave us flu medication. Howard died of peritonitis on December fourteenth. The following February, the first sulpha drugs were successfully administered. These are the things that my poem "Such a Child's Waiting" does not tell.

Christine was born in 1937 and the next year another was stillborn. But before this, also in 1936, the Rural Electrification Act brought modern conveniences to our area. Four years later, during a gale force wind, the great overland barn, having been ineptly wired, caught fire and every building except this house went up in flames. And with these our marriage. I left my husband's bed.

There was so much warmth and neighborliness in those difficult weeks and strangers were supportive, why do I relate the dark side? Perhaps to exorcise myself of it —finally: though I pleaded and wept and threatened, an ugly high barn was built below this house, shutting off with its board wind-break the entire eastern view (a tornado removed these and much else in 1972, two months after Peter's death).

To the north, where I had looked out across thousands of dishwashings, like Ernest in Hawthorne's "The Great Stone Face," to beautiful Blue Mounds, went an eighty-foot machine shed. For my vista-seeking eyes there was left only the cowled hills to the southwest and a flat road toward Dodgeville, somewhat obscured by the old orchard and a grove of sapling locusts.

Though Peter knew my caring about these, I came home one day from a PTA foodstand stint during a music festival to find them all bulldozed down and burning. For more cropland, I was told. Next, the road was rerouted so as to create a single field. I tried to see the sense in that, since tractors and larger machinery made triangular plots obsolete. Even so, it was ill-conceived: this winter it will cost five-hundred thirty dollars for snow removal through the dips (like weak links in a chain?) in that road leading to the highway. Sitting here alone, I remember those other silences.

Silences? Devastating silences that are so like drought, parching foliage and roots, ruining a landscape of life. I sometimes think that now when there is such abuse-awareness, it is the hate that dare not speak its name—so little attention is given this silent treatment that renders the victim a non-person.

Two instances come to mind. When the burned barn was to be replaced, Peter wanted a hundred and ten foot structure. The beams for the framework and the lumber were to come from my parents' farm then being rented by Leo and family. Such wood must come mostly from virgin timber. A building of that size would have practically denuded the farm my brother was to inherit. Neither Father nor Leo wanted that to happen. They agreed to *give* us an eighty-foot barn frame, siding, etc. We paid only for the labor of cutting down the oak trees, the sawing and millwork. . . .

Peter did not speak to either of them from the end of April until Christmas day. Likewise, his silence sent Richard into World War II before he was eighteen. In both cases, the relationships were blighted and he reaped the bitterest harvest.

At these times, instead of being angry, frustrated and stubborn, blind to his inability to change, I might have been compassionate and helpful, and not as many years later I could describe Peter and I, in "Fiery-Eyed the Bittersweet," the poem for my son:

> This poem is meant to tell of single lives
> humdrum inhumanities, of battle scenes beyond
> the sites of wars where no mediator dares to enter,
> how we who gave you life took a tollway
> years and years and years in length
> and killed each other a little every day.

My angers were like summer storms—fast, explosive, and soon spent, often leaving with cruel words, damage as aftermath. Fortunately, as in nature's storms, clemency followed times to mend and clear. I have used the past tense for the reason there is little virtue in equaninimity acquired with age. It may be true that we care less, but our view has broadened and a kind of wisdom rises out of the unknown.

Today, I am here in sunlight and boisterous wind, I do not know how near to the end of this journey. I will likely see these fields silky green with seeding alfalfa, sepia with whispering corn. I have come far but not yet to where one contemplates life as from an uppermost steep, nor am I weighted with moods of going "down into the darkling valley," though I have in the same spirit set my financial house in order: bequests, scholarships, last will and testament. For half a century I have loved this home, its fascicle of contents too dear for recounting, though none more so that the rose jar. These are my reality, the leit-motif of my life.

Under the clutter of years I can hear the heart of a three-year-old taking her first steps, of the frightened girl giving home-birth to her first son, the stopped heart of the young woman when love entered her life, the heart breaking over and over with each death. Placed as I was between duty and dreams it is unlikely, if wits endure, I will forget the helpless misery of a young wife. For it makes this loneliness and the physical pain, of which I do not speak, insignificant. I never understood Christmas—the date is wrong: shepherds are not in the fields of Judea after autumn equinox. I have never been to Bethlehem. Obviously Jesus liked it no better than I the Valley. He never went back to his birthplace. I do understand the vagaries of April, so like life. I am reasonably happy and have joy for sharing. I have lived Lent and Easter. Born on the day of the Feast of Golgotha, I *know* the way of the Cross.

Years ago I wrote of "The Beginning of Wisdom: —about that interim farm near Ridgeway. It makes an appropriate closing to this book.

Edna with her dog Rex (Dale Stuerman photo)

The Beginning of Wisdom

That bitter April when fires were to fend the chill
they mined the frozen ground like coal to put you in.
Nor was the sun for warming leafless trees, or me.
The moon's dark side in quarter peel stood by,
and I impervious to searching eyes, to pelting sleet
recalled first touch: Your kiss like struck match
to underbrush that burns a woodland clean.

Today I passed the farmstead—fenceless and merged—
our interim home, that center of care—a sagging
reliquary, for tearing down.
Who seeing the house or me grown old, believe such glow
as lit the shores of Troy, the sky at Peshtigo
illumined us here? Life is that but once.

My finite mind blocked now by concept of infinity,
unable to imagine where spirit goes, took then
in certitude as due a sustenance of bliss.

I, who cannot ascertain the sun we know is there,
conceive a habitat for what still lives of you,
recall how, Atlased with prides, I dared to doubt
an afterlife while you were here and god in mine.
And THIS I think, the SUN of suns and other worlds,
of life must find for clemency the least desert,
for want of wisdom the sorriest excuse.